DOGS

Heart-Warming, Soul-Stirring Stories of Our Canine Companions

John Cali

BookLocker.com, Inc.
Bangor, Maine
http://www.BookLocker.com

DOGS

Heart-Warming, Soul-Stirring Stories of Our Canine Companions

John Cali

Library of Congress Control Number: 2007906733

© 2008 John Cali

ISBN-13 978-0-924033-44-5
ISBN-10 0-92403-44-4

Printed in the United States of America

Published by: BookLocker.com, Inc.
                 Bangor, Maine

Cover design by Todd Engel

Dedication

This book is dedicated to those humans everywhere who love and care for dogs who also care for them. God could not have chosen a greater gift for humanity than to grace our lives with these wonderful, magical, uninhibited creatures. They unconditionally give their all, and ask little in return.

And so this book is dedicated also to those creatures who bring so much joy, pleasure, love, and healing into our lives.

We dedicate this book also to all people involved in the healing, caring, and nurturing of dogs: the veterinary professionals, the selfless souls who give their resources to help countless homeless dogs, members of the many organizations dedicated to dog welfare, and to all those advocates for the rights of dogs and all animals, including the many unsung anonymous heroes who give so much love in so many ways to our animal families.

Although we don't see much "good" news in the mainstream news media, there are far more acts of kindness and love in our world today than there are acts of "evil." We need only to look to the dogs' good deeds to see that.

I would love to see the world "go to the dogs."

Table of Contents

Acknowledgments

So many people contributed, directly and indirectly, to this book. No book is the work of only the author or editor. It's a collaborative venture, and involves many "behind-the-scenes" folks. I want to express my heartfelt gratitude to the following people who, knowingly or unknowingly, helped make this book a reality.

My parents, John and Mary Cali, whose Fourth of July gift to their children was our first dog. I was only nine years old. Blackie, a mutt of doubtful heritage, lived fifteen years. Over those years, Blackie taught me much, and I fell head-over-heels in love with dogs. So thank you, Mom and Dad. And you too, Blackie.

Angela and Richard Hoy, owners and publishers of Booklocker.com, Inc., for their patient guidance and wise counsel in the creating and publishing of this book.

Suzanne Keyes, my dear friend, for giving me the idea and the inspiration for this book, and for her constant support in the writing of it.

My family, including John Cali III, my son, who shares my great love for dogs, and who wrote the story of Wily in this book. John's mother, Theresa Cali, who brought Wily into our lives. Ingrid Cali whose 1990 birthday gift to me was Schnapsi, our beloved miniature schnauzer.

Scott Moore, D.V.M., my Wyoming friend and veterinarian, who lovingly cared for Schnapsi, until Schnapsi's unexpectedly early death.

Joan Bramsch and Judee Pouncey, my dear friends, for their unparalleled writing and editing expertise and guidance.

Alf Wight, known to the world as James Herriot, the beloved British North Yorkshire veterinarian of *All Creatures Great and Small* fame. Dogs were Alf's favorite animals, and his many touching dog stories have for years been a great inspiration to me.

Dan Poynter of Para Publishing, my friend, mentor, and publisher extraordinaire, for his wise advice and counsel over many years.

All the dogs in our family over the years. Each one, with its unique personality, has brought much joy, love, and healing into my life and into the lives of my family.

The wonderful writers and dog lovers who contributed to this book. Without them, the book would not have happened.

I am deeply grateful to all of you.

With love and appreciation,
John

Introduction

I was shopping recently in a local store. Just after I arrived, one of the young ladies who works there came in with her dog. Life is pretty informal here in this little Wyoming town. As in Europe, people don't mind if you bring your dog into a store.

The dog was a tiny black bundle of fur—she was about eight or nine inches tall, and couldn't have weighed more than three or four pounds. What she lacked in size, however, she more than made up for in her boundless energy.

As soon as she spotted me, she came running up, bright eyes sparkling with joy through her thick black eyebrows. She stood on her hind legs, front paws on my knee, with a big smile on her face, tail wagging furiously. She was adorable. Obviously, she loved people—everyone, it seemed, since she greeted each new customer in the same friendly manner.

She filled the whole store with her energy and love. People were smiling and laughing, even with other folks they didn't know.

This tiny creature instantly, magically transformed the whole place. The shift in energy was dramatic and all felt it. Their faces suddenly lit up with joy and happiness, as if they were once again little children.

Such is the power of unbridled love and joy. Dogs uplift us, make us smile, and let us know we are loved.

The following excerpts from a book by the late Rev. Diane K. Chapin give us a more spiritual perspective of our animal companions. Diane's words are a wonderful tribute to dogs, and to all pets.[1]

---

[1] Our gratitude goes to Rev. Don Chapin, Ph.D. for his permission to use these excerpts. Visit Don's Web site, Light Path Resources - World Wide, at: http://www.lprww.us/.

Pets come in with the singular purpose of displaying spirituality for you in its highest form. That is, they live in the moment, they provide unconditional love, they honor themselves and you at all times.

Pets live connected to other souls rather than in a disconnected state as so many human entities do. They are literally lights of Spirit on earth and that is how they should be viewed by you. They are illuminated to the fullest of their capability, which is truly what spirituality is about—to be illuminated to the fullest of their capability—of your capability. In other words, they honor Spirit at all times.

...those animals who come into your life for a lengthy period of time are literally vibrationally attuned to you. They come in on a wave of upliftment and grace into your very home to bring you an aspect of love and contentment that you may be lacking in other areas of your life. This is why these beings come into your life.

This is how you should be serving one another: with unconditional love, with unquestioned reverence for the divinity of one another. This is what they see and this is what their message is to you: that they will love you unconditionally until their deaths, but that, so too, should you love one another unconditionally and see the Spirit of divinity that is behind the eyes of all souls....The pet sees through ego, personality and selfishness to that which is the essence of all beings.

Please enjoy these heart-warming, soul-stirring stories of some of the most enchanting and quirky canines you'll ever meet.

Dog Tales

Happiness is a warm puppy.

Charles M. Schulz

A few days ago, my ten-month-old puppy, Zelda (who, yes, like F. Scott Fitzgerald's wife, must, on a regular basis, be locked up) decided to take an unauthorized tour of the neighborhood. She escaped from me as I was attempting to put her outside on her chain. I had just gotten home from work and was still dressed in my work clothes, complete with pantyhose and red high heels. As she dashed down the driveway and across the street, I followed her as quickly as possible, a demented Dorothy in ruby slippers trying to retrieve a very poorly behaved Toto.

Zelda was not trying to run over the rainbow, but rather indulge in a neighborhood-wide game of "Chase." Looking over her shoulder she would let me get almost close enough to touch her, and then she would bound out of reach. It was a great entertainment for my neighbors, who, for some reason or another, were reluctant to join in the game. Well, it could be the fact Zelda often appears with a muzzle on (a vain attempt to discourage constant barking and grass-eating) or perhaps the huge "Beware of Dog" sign on my house, meant to discourage unwanted visitors when I am not home.

My neighbors stood behind their fences, laughing and pointing as Zelda, a golden retriever mix with a huge tail held up like a flag, raced back and forth, with me hobbling after her in my workday finery and red shoes. Finally, I was able to corner her against a fence and drag her disobedient furry butt home. She immediately drank an entire bowl of water, and collapsed on the floor, with an expression on her face that clearly said, "Now that was fun."

She had the same look on her face when it was discovered she had chewed my daughter's entire wardrobe of underwear, an act that clearly warned the dangers of leaving unattended laundry baskets on the floor. It's an expression Zelda sports anytime one discovers her chewing on things she shouldn't, such as vacuum cleaner cords and watchbands. To add to the aggravation, she usually has her own dog

3

toy right next to the illegal object, as if to say, "Oops, I chewed the wrong thing."

Having this puppy in the house brings back memories of all the dog mischief I have been subjected to my entire life. Now some families are not dog families and cannot comprehend why we are willing to subject ourselves to this. To those families all I can say is you haven't lived until you come home to find your house has been gleefully redecorated with the fragrant contents of your kitchen garbage can. Or the family is reduced to sitting on folding chairs to watch television because the couch belongs to the dog.

However, if you are a dog family, you understand the joy and companionship far outweigh the chewed-up camera straps and stained carpeting. And the stories of the dogs that spend their lives with you become the stuff of family legend.

The dog I grew up with was a good-natured basset hound named The Red Baron. A show dog with a championship bloodline, I occasionally would show him in the Junior Showmanship section of American Kennel Club dog shows. Unlike the professional dogs who arrived in crates with fancy grooming tables, Red would ride in the car like one of the kids, his paws resting on the back of the front seat and his nose constantly knocking off my father's hat. This was also the lazy, slow-moving dog who, at the mere mention of bedtime, would be off like a shot, flying up the stairs as fast as his short little legs would carry him. If you weren't able to catch up with him, he would jump in your bed first, settle in the exact middle with his head on the pillow, forcing you to sleep, blanketless, on the edge.

Later, as a single young woman living alone, I felt the need for a dog not only for companionship but protection. This was naturally what I was looking for when I fell for a miniature daschund in a pet store. I named him Max, after the song "Maxwell's Silver Hammer." I can't explain why I felt the need to name my dog after a musical serial killer; however, I think he took it very seriously. Max was the only schizophrenic dog I have ever had, and all I can say is, thank goodness he only weighed five pounds.

At certain times, Max would station himself under a chair and attack anything that passed by, including my feet. Attempts to clip his nails induced a mania that required three people to control. And once, while romping in the yard at my parent's house, he bit down on a stick so hard, the ends snapped off, leaving the middle of the stick firmly lodged against the roof of his mouth. It took the entire family to hold him down, open his mouth, and yank out the stick. He promptly rewarded my father by sinking his teeth into his hand. Biting the hand that fed him was Max's hobby.

Gypsy was the dog who served as the "first child" when I was married. A devoted and well- trained German shepherd, she was popular in our circle of friends. But friends are in short supply when your dog goes out in the yard and meets a skunk. No one wants to come over and help you douse her with tomato juice, orange juice, baby powder, and vinegar. Kids run away screaming, slamming their bedroom doors and yelling "She's not sleeping in here tonight!" So much for all her years of loyalty.

Now we have Zelda. Born in a junkyard and bottle-fed by a kindly family who rescued her from a malnourished mother, Zelda still feels the need to be cuddled and held. The problem is, she is almost fifty pounds, with a tail that would be more appropriate for a horse. Days and nights are spent keeping her body off the furniture, her paws off guests, her head out of the fish bowl, and her tail away from anything not nailed down. Her extreme distractibility means she often takes a drink of water, forgets to swallow it, and proceeds to dribble it all over the first person she encounters.

I've been trying hard to come up with a solution that keeps Zelda occupied and doesn't involve house demolition. Finally, yesterday, I turned down a road I don't usually take, and passed a huge facility called Canine Academy. There, behind sturdy, tall fencing was an elaborate dog obstacle course, complete with things to jump over, squeeze under, crawl through, and run around. The perfect place for Zelda and her Olympic-style dog tricks. I made a mental note to call the school right away and get information on how she can join in.

Just as soon as I catch her.

Noreen Braman

More Than "Just A Dog"

No matter how little money and how few possessions you own, having a dog makes you rich.

Louis Sabin

Don't console Helen Stout by telling her the German shepherd she's grieving was "just a dog." Helen, fifty-seven, lost something dear when Baron died this month.

She brought him home to Lower Makefield ten years ago. Baron lived for walks, car rides, doggie treats, and Helen's attention. Her husband would say, "Helen, he's a dog." But she didn't pay him any mind. She loved that animal.

Not because he was heroic or remarkable, though he was, in Helen's eyes, a darling.

"Everyone who knew him liked him," she said. Even the UPS guy whom Baron would escort up the walk. Helen would open the door and there they'd be, man and beast.

Baron was 110 pounds. It's hard to say if the UPS man liked Baron or was just grateful Baron didn't eat him.

I wouldn't wonder about this to Helen. She called Baron her "beloved companion." She is a head-over-heels dog lover. Just like dog enthusiast George G. Vest. He's the guy who said:

> The one absolutely unselfish friend that a man can have in this selfish world, the one that never deserts him and the one that never proves ungrateful or treacherous is his dog....He will kiss the hand that has no food to offer, he will lick the wounds and sores

that come in encounters with the roughness of the world....When all other friends desert, he remains.[2]

But I tell Rachel Canelli, the young woman who sits in the cubicle next to me, that George G. Vest is full of soup.

All dogs aren't as loyal as some want us to believe. If they were, mine wouldn't pee on a neighbor's front lawn just as the neighbor is pulling into her driveway.

Not all dogs are loyal, easy friends like Baron. It's a lie we should stop telling each other.

I tell Rachel this so she won't cry at her desk. Maddie, the mix of Shar-Pei and God-knows-what Rachel and husband Mike rescued from the pound, ran away last week. Out the doggy door, over the electric fence, the little purple and pink bandana flapping in the breeze.

Rachel feels she lost more than "just a dog."

She and Mike put up fliers, put an ad in the paper, knocked on doors, called the animal control officer and the SPCA. Maddie, with more wanderlust than good sense, was last seen near Crooked Billet Elementary School in Hatboro. If you have her, Rachel and Mike want her back. Very much.

That's funny, when you hear how Maddie pooped on the carpet, hopped on the bed, and chewed the stuffing right out of the love seat. They loved her. Played ball with her, cuddled her, cut a hole in the wall for that doggy door so she wouldn't feel cooped up.

Maybe she met up with Brutus. He's missing, too. A white English bulldog last seen near New Falls Road and the Levittown Parkway, according to the ad, which reads, "Family devastated."

Aw, it's just a dog, non-dog lovers say.

Just a dog.

---

[2] George Vest was a 19th century lawyer and United States Senator. This quote is from a closing argument he made in the trial of a man who had killed a neighbor's dog. The argument has come to be known as "Eulogy to a Dog." It was part of Shep's eulogy in the chapter "Forever Faithful: Shep's Story."

That is what my sister called Sigmund, the ugliest Boston terrier you ever did see. A nuisance, she told her husband and daughter after they brought Sigmund home. For years, she grumbled as she fed him and played with him and carried him across the snow to a dry place where he could do his business. Ziggy hated the snow, and my sister swore she didn't much like Ziggy, but she carried him anyway.

And when Ziggy, like Baron, got old and sick and died, my sister held Ziggy's face and wept. Just a dog. Just a dog. And something more.

Kate Fratti

Remembering Alice

Children and dogs are as necessary to the welfare of the country as Wall Street and the railroads.

Harry S. Truman

Alice was a full-blooded Doberman with a healthy dose of great Dane, or so it seemed. She stood as tall as a grown man's waist, and tipped the scales at over one hundred pounds of sleek, lean muscle. She and her chosen human lived in the little town of Marble, high in the Colorado Rockies. Back in the 70s, long before the town became a chic artist's village, there was one main street and only a few year-round businesses. Everyone in town knew each other, and everyone knew Alice. She wasn't a normal dog. In fact, she was an anomaly by abnormal standards. An entertainer and an annoyance, she was a dog you couldn't help but love—or hate. There was no neutral ground. For better or for worse, she was a local legend.

Alice was a human trapped in a canine body. She truly believed she was a person, and expected to be treated with the proper regard. She loved human food, human conversation, and human entertainment. One of her primary hobbies was to travel in cars. She would sit tall in the passenger seat, like any other person. Unfortunately, she wasn't terribly choosy about whose car to grace with her presence. If a resident or guest left the car window open, they might return from shopping or visiting to find Alice sitting in the car, waiting for her owner to take her for an outing. And only her owner would do. May God help you if you tried to enter your own car. It had suddenly become her territory, and she would defend it vigorously.

Defending property was a skill she honed to a razor-sharp edge. Her territory was *her* territory. Once, a business owner came to call on the other occupant of Alice's house to make a job offer. Work was scarce, and the money was sorely needed. Alice was asleep on the porch steps when he arrived, or so it seemed. The man innocently

9

mounted the steps, placing one foot on the tread below Alice, and one above, so as not to disturb her. This was a mistake. She rose as though propelled by rockets, all fangs, saliva, and noise. She didn't hurt the visitor, but you could almost see her chuckle as he ran in air frantically, to descend heavily on the landing. Her job done, she lay back down quietly to wait for the next diversion.

Amusing oneself is important in a small town. Unlike most of the local dogs, Alice didn't chase cars. She shunned them as beneath her dignity. At the speeds required by the town laws, they weren't a challenge to her long legs and powerful muscles. Few rabbits can live at that elevation, so she needed more suitable entertainment; something fast, maneuverable, canny. The perfect challenge presented itself in the form of children on bicycles. She would wait patiently until they reached the far edge of her property, then would race after them, zigging and zagging across road and yard until she caught a pant cuff and pulled them off. There was no malice, no harm intended. Alice wouldn't maul them; not even truly threaten them. She would simply leap joyously over the tangle of body and metal and speed off after the next prey.

The local parents were outraged, incensed. They demanded the owner fence her up, or chain her down. But how do you confine a dog that can break the biggest chain, can leap the highest fence? Her owner refused. Not-so-quietly he suggested the children stay away from his property, since she would not stray far from home. The parents were appalled, and sought the sheriff. In true mountain spirit, he agreed with the owner. She was not vicious, and only defended her territory. He, too, suggested their children stay away.

The children knew but didn't care about their parents' concerns. They had found a sport, and its name was Alice. There was no thrill greater than speeding past her and denying her the catch. No adrenalin surge as intoxicating. There were giggles and screams of delight as she caught them and brought them down. They would ride by the house, calling for her to join the game. These were not city children, who needed to be protected from the world. Mountain children are a hardier breed. I sometimes wonder whether some grownup child on the Tour de France or Ride the Rockies still has visions of glossy fur and gaping jaws just behind his or her back heel. The church had no greater friend than Alice. The one and only church in Marble was directly across the street from Alice's home. Every Sunday, the church bells would call the faithful to worship. Alice didn't like bells. When they started to ring, she would trot across the street and perch on the church steps, underneath the bells, where the sound was less. After all the people were seated she became a guardian. With bared teeth and a low growl, she would block the path of anyone attempting to leave early. In fact, she would often trap the entire congregation of parishioners for extra prayer time if she felt it appropriate. She considered the church and grounds to be part of her territory, and she had the right to defend it against the weekly intruders.

She had a sweet side, and a sweet tooth. Grandma's peanut butter cookies were the way to her heart. For peanut butter cookies, she would renounce her basic nature. She would beg, grovel, even (gasp!) do tricks for the merest crumb. She liked warm fires in the cold winter, and the gentle attention of loving hands.

Alice had an unerring sense of people. She knew only her instincts, and had no reason to trust in a person's words over them. If she disliked a person, there was usually a reason. Whatever made her uneasy about a person might come to light that day, or twenty years later, but she was always proven right.

For all her faults, Alice was the best pet an owner could hope for. She was a good dog. She had moods and tempers, and took joy in the world around her. As with all things in life, Alice left Marble when her owner moved. The town never saw the likes of her again. It's been many years, and Alice has surely passed on—hopefully living forever in the sky, chasing phantom bikers and eating sun-baked peanut butter cookies. That's all a dog can hope for.

Cathy Clamp

11

My Search for Beau

The bond with a dog is as lasting as the ties of this Earth can ever be.

Konrad Lorenz

EDITOR'S NOTE: *This story, obviously, is atypical of the other stories in the book. We've included it because we believe it clearly and poignantly demonstrates the deep love many of us have for our canine companions.*

On July 1, 2003 I arrived home from work a little earlier than usual. This particular day I drove along the top of our sloping property instead of driving down the driveway to the verandah where Beau and Jessie, my English setters, stayed when I was away at work. Even though the entire five acres of our property is securely fenced and electrified and the front gate to the property is always locked, I never allowed my dogs to run free inside our property when I was either away from home or not with them, to ensure no harm came to them in any way.

I parked the car near the back door and went immediately into the house. I missed my dogs (and horses) just as much as they missed me. As I headed towards the verandah, I became panic-stricken. I could not see either Beau or Jessie. Beau would normally be standing upright with his paws on the sliding door, tearing at the screen, crying out to me, telling me how much he had missed me. And Jessie would be standing right beside Beau, wagging her tail furiously.

I ran to the door and then I saw Jessie. She was sitting on one of their doggie beds. I opened the door and raced over to her. Jessie was shaking. She was traumatized. I knelt down and placed my arms around her and held her close. Jessie then looked up at me with the saddest eyes I had ever seen, gulped, and placed her paw over my arm. Then she buried her head in my heart, and she cried.

I felt sick to the core of my being. I knew something terribly bad had happened on the verandah this day while I was away at work. *Beau was gone!*

After Jessie had settled, I left her on the doggie bed and walked around the verandah in disbelief. There was no way Beau could have escaped from this verandah. It was 2½ meters high (over eight feet). The gate at the top of the stairs was still bolted. Then I stared in disbelief, as a chair had been moved right away from the table and was sitting flush against the wall. Neither Beau nor Jessie could have moved the chair to this position.

I was consumed with complete and utter despair.

My gut feeling was someone had been on the verandah with my beloved Beau and Jessie this day while I was not at home to protect them. Beau and Jessie are gentle dogs. They could not defend themselves against a human. They would not know how. They would not hurt a fly. Wild birds have made their home on our property and I feed these birds. These birds sit beside my dogs. We are all a family together. We love each other and we protect each other.

I took action immediately, phoning veterinary practices and dog pounds, talking to all the neighbors, driving the streets until very late that night calling out Beau's name. I started again at daybreak the next morning, searching the neighbors' properties, driving the streets looking for Beau. By the end of the day I had distributed Beau's flyer to 200 acreage properties in the local neighborhood as well as to many businesses—the local hotel, the garbage tip, produce stores, video stores, too many to name. The next day I started advertising in newspapers and I have not stopped.

I could not begin to tell you what I have done, where I have traveled, whom I have spoken to, desperately searching for Beau. Because of the extent and the depth of my search, I know now Beau did not escape from the verandah on July 1, 2003.

As I write this, the date is July 17, 2006. More than three years have passed since this terrible day. Beau was two years and five months old the day he was stolen. He is now almost five years and six months old. I have not seen my boy in all this time. He was just starting to mature physically when he was stolen. I do not know exactly what Beau looks like now but I would know my boy immediately out of one hundred English setters, and Beau would know I was coming for him, even before he saw me. The bond of love between Beau and me will never be broken. Our love for each other will span eternity.

People continually tell me to "move on." They do not understand I have to get on with my life for Beau's family and for Beau. However, this does not mean I have to abandon my search for Beau. I will never stop searching for Beau until I know he is safe.

People continually tell me Beau is with a loving family and I should leave him where he is. They are saying these words for themselves, so they feel comfortable with themselves. These words do not help me and most importantly, they do not help Beau, or all the other lost dogs like Beau.

I do not know where Beau is and how he is being cared for. Humans who stalk other humans, trespass into their homes, and steal a very beloved member of their family, have no respect for life. How can I have any confidence Beau is being cared for well? I cannot. How can I abandon my search for Beau, despite the intense emotional strain and the financial strain, knowing he is not safe? I cannot.

My search for Beau has consumed my life for the last three years. At the same time I try to ensure as best as I can that the rest of my family does not suffer because what has happened to Beau is not their fault. I pretend to be strong and happy. I play games with them. However, they all know and understand the deep despair I feel deep inside my heart and soul for Beau.

Many humans think animals are stupid, have limited feelings, and are not spiritual. Some humans think animals don't go to heaven when they die. I believe animals are far superior to humans in every way.

I purchased Hobson, who is also an English setter, sight unseen, at three days of age. Hobson was born on June 10, 2003, three weeks before Beau was stolen. Hobson flew all the way from Tasmania to the Gold Coast at only eight weeks of age. He arrived in a Dogtainers® pet carrier[3]. Even at this young age, Hobson knew something was wrong.

---

[3] "Dogtainers" is a term coined by the Australian pet transport company of the same name, and registered as a US trademark.

Hobson decided his place in the car was sitting on the console between the two front seats beside his mum. Our car is a four-wheel-drive Jeep Cherokee and the back seats are folded down to give my dogs plenty of room. Hobson still sits on this console even though he is now three years old and he weighs thirty-three kilograms (about seventy-three pounds). His bottom just manages to fit and his front legs extend to the passenger's seat. He delights everyone when they see him sitting proudly beside his mum. Hobson has spent a major part of his life searching for his brother Beau. He knows he has a brother even though he has not seen him yet.

I am a very sensitive, gentle person and I have always found it extremely difficult dealing with the harshness of life. By "harshness," I don't mean challenges. I mean the terrible cruelty humans are capable of. I cry so hard when I see an animal being mistreated, or a child, or an old person, any being who is innocent and unable to defend herself or himself. I come home and I hold my dogs and my horses and I know they are safe, except for Beau. He is not safe. He is at the mercy of whatever human has him. No matter what I do so far, I cannot find my beloved Beau.

No one in Australia has ever searched for a lost dog as long as I have, borrowed as much money, spent as much time, and most importantly, willingly sacrificed as much as I have. Beau is not "just a dog" to me. He is my family. He is my boy. He is my friend, my defender, my dog. He loves me unconditionally with all my imperfections. He helped me to recover from a serious illness. He has made me laugh even in moments of despair. He has given me immeasurable love and devotion.

I could not just put up a cardboard sign on a tree, distribute a few flyers, visit a few pounds and shelters, mourn my loss for Beau, and then move on. My boy Beau is not safe. I have to find him before he dies. I will have no peace in my life until I know Beau is safe and he is back home with us again.

My search for Beau has attracted national media attention in Australia numerous times and the media attention is continuing after three years. Unfortunately, the majority of the media exposure has focused on money instead of the real issues. I continue to receive a backlash and this also happens with my advertising. Despite the constant threats, ridicule, and criticism, no one will ever make me stop searching for Beau.

People continue to rip down Beau's posters and I hammer them up somewhere else. They continue to throw away Beau's flyers and I display them somewhere else. I feel sick inside when I receive obscene phone calls, letters, and emails, particularly when they come from women. But I gather up my strength, not for myself, for Beau. I am fifty-five years old and I'm in more debt now than ever in my life. I do not regret in any way what I have done to try to find Beau.

In my search for Beau I have met the very best and the very worst of people, and everything in between. The contrast in human nature is mind-boggling.

As time goes on my Web site is reaching more and more like-minded people who are joining my cause. This has restored my faith there are a lot of good people in this world who respect all life. They care about a goofy-faced English setter whose name is Beau, whom they do not even know. They are doing everything they can to help me find him.

My love for Beau has touched people's hearts around the world. One lady in the United Kingdom was so touched, she displayed Beau's flyers in her local village to let people know about Beau and she asked them to send positive wishes and prayers into the Universe to bring Beau safely back home. Another lady who lives in Sydney sent me a hand-carved statue of Archangel Michael she brought from the holy city of Medugorje in Bosnia-Hercegovina to support my prayers for Beau's safe return. Little children crowd around me when they see me with my English setters. They are so disappointed when I tell them Beau is still away from home. Many men have wept openly because they understand my love for Beau.

Among us all, I believe we will find Beau.

"The hurt of one is the hurt of all. The honor of one is the honor of all." These words are profound and mean a great deal to me. They are from a book titled *The Sacred Tree*, a handbook of Native American Spirituality, by Julie Bopp, Michael Bopp, Lee Brown, and Phil Lane.

The hurt of Beau is the hurt of all. The honor of Beau is the honor of all. There is not a happy ending to my story yet, but there will be in the next edition.

Susan Dennis

EDITOR'S NOTE: *As of our publishing date, Susan has not yet found Beau.*

Always Look on the Bright Side

Happiness to a dog is what lies on the other side of a door.
                                                    Charleton Ogburn Jr.

Sometimes, it's hard to be funny. Of course, in times of national tragedy and disaster humorists not only have difficulty finding the funny perspective; they walk a fine line between providing stress relief and offending someone. Bill Maher[4] found that out the hard way after September 11, 2001, but I am not talking about dealing with global events. Sometimes, daily life just makes it hard to be funny. Yet, nothing helps maintain a cool head or provides a better perspective than finding humor in the situation.

This lesson in finding humor starts with my dog. Zelda[5] has already provided an entire column of witty anecdotes, but this month she proved her value as more than the house clown. I came home to find her with her nose pushed under the stove, imitating the heavy breathing of Darth Vader. She was pawing at the underside of the kitchen cabinet and whining. I knew this meant probably a microscopic fleck of dog food had rolled under the stove and the smell of it had Zelda convinced I was hiding a whole side of beef under there.

I pulled out the stove to let her find this out-of-reach treasure, but she continued to paw at the adjoining cabinet. A cabinet that looked strangely out of plumb without the stove next to it; a cabinet that suddenly had an open space under it where the kick plate was supposed to fit. Now, that's funny, I thought.

Thinking perhaps an opportunistic mouse had squeezed under the cabinet and was swishing its tail just out of the reach of Zelda's nose

---

[4] Bill Maher is an American talk show host known for his political satire and social commentary.

[5] The author talked about Zelda in an earlier chapter, "Dog Tales."

and paws, I bravely inserted a flashlight in the hole to see what, if anything, was under the cabinet.

No mice at that point, probably because they would be unable to balance on thin air—under my cabinet was a gaping hole, and cold air was rushing through it. The bottom of my kitchen cabinet was sagging into the chasm, and I was immediately reminded of the scene from "Poltergeist"[6] when the whole house is sucked down into the ground. Removal of the cabinets revealed lots of rotten flooring, centered around a brand-new water meter that was gently spritzing the area with water.

At least my homeowner's insurance company immediately took the situation seriously. In response to my call asking what to do, I got a warm and fuzzy form letter telling me a representative would be contacting me soon, and I should be sure to protect the property from further damage.

The water company, whose leaky meter (installed by them in 2000 and, mostly likely, leaking since that time) may play a significant role in this. They assured me someone might be out to evaluate the damage in two weeks. When I offered to assuage their concern for me and my family by offering to move to a hotel at their expense for the duration, I was reminded, "Well, you do have water."

Oh yes, no shortage of that, especially since the water company repairmen, assigned to contain the leak only, were unable to shut off the main, for fear of breaking the old valve in the street in front of my house. Of course, getting water when your sink has fallen into the crawlspace can be difficult. But after all, I still had the bathroom sink.

Several days later, uncharacteristic wetness in the bathroom pointed out the fact the bathroom vanity was attempting to flee the room, and cracked a pipe in the attempt. Probably fearing dropping down into the crawlspace too, the sink was waving one of its cabinet doors toward a crack in the wall next to the bathtub. And there was Zelda, crying and pawing at the gap, as the suddenly spongy floor underneath her gently rippled up and down. It would appear, after fifty years of perfect posture, my house had decided to relax a bit.

---

[6] Steven Spielberg's horror movie of the early 1980s.

Now I am walking carefully after replacing eight feet of kitchen floor, and discovering a rotten joist under there. I wonder which part of the floor will cave in next. Will I be in the shower, naked and singing opera, when the floor gives way? My children have explicit instructions that if this happens, they are to call the fire department to rescue me, but only after they have climbed down in the hole and dressed me. The firemen are not getting a naked lady rescue story out of me, that's for sure. If anyone gets funny stories to tell about this adventure, it's going to be me.

Noreen Braman

Monty

Dogs are our link to paradise. They don't know evil or jealousy or discontent. To sit with a dog on a hillside on a glorious afternoon is to be back in Eden, where doing nothing was not boring—it was peace.

Milan Kundera

We are a "cat" family, Monty. I think you always knew that, and dedicated your life to proving to us there was the possibility of canine superiority.

Do you remember when we met? You were the self-assured pup sitting patiently in the corner of the cage as your brothers and sisters yipped their misery. You were the terrier-mix fluff ball in the group with intelligent eyes. Something in them met mine—I think it was kindness I saw—and when I left the store, I had you in my arms.

We had two little girls at home, and two grown cats. I thought it important the girls grow up with a dog. You see, my personal commitment to you was altruistic—for them—and rather superficial. You would fit in, but you would be the girls' pet.

Well. The tears that ran freely when it occurred to me you might not survive your recent paralysis came from a deep well of affection our years together have honed. My blatant sobs and aching heart as we buried you beneath the juniper were testament to the attachment we shared for each other over twelve years. There is an empty place in my day for you, Monty. The lump in my throat when I think of our times together has not gone away. I know time will change that. It always does. Today, though, I want to tell you what you came to mean to me—what you taught me.

You were a terrier mix—black fluff with golden markings and penetrating black eyes. We did not consider docking your tail or clipping your ears. You were a warm and cuddly shaggy dog in the winter, and a smartly clipped schnauzer-looking piece of elegance in the summer and fall. Yes, we had you clipped. We, who cut our own

21

daughters' hair to save at the beauty shop, paid tightly budgeted dollars to have your easily matted shag cut. Though you stepped out smartly with each new clip, secretly, you and I both preferred the comfort of your familiar and friendly shaggy-dog hair. That is how you were laid to rest. Familiar and friendly, I am happy that is our last memory together.

Do you remember how little you were? You could walk underneath the cats and nip at their bellies. Their nose-in-the-air attempt to ignore you was wasted. Your enthusiasm to be the friendly newcomer vaulted you to eminence with your persistent determination to be part of the family.

You were a quick study. You were trained within days, eager to please at every turn. Your feelings could be bruised with a look. I feel guilty, Monty, that we used that sensitive nature of yours to fit you into our lifestyle. And, fit in, you did. You were not built like a runner, but you were an apt and capable one. Do you remember the girls racing ahead on a country road while we held you? You loved the game, and caught them and passed them—barking your victory— each and every time. And, as I think of you now, I envision a little black ball, ears flying, chasing her girls in a high mountain meadow.

Wherever you are now, I hope you are running out your joy in an amiable meadow, chasing along with the wind lifting your ears.

Your girls learned so much from you. You were always an eager and affable companion to them. You taught them responsibility for another creature, rewarding their efforts with face-licking enthusiasm. When they were older, they would take you on your favorite "bye-bye" trips. Sometimes it was just a trip to the store; other times, they included you in their personal camping and hiking trips. Thank you for enriching the souls of our daughters, Monty.

I think of the countless times you would sit outside with me, on the ground, and lean into me for support. Physical closeness was bliss to you. You would sit for hours while I read or gardened or did what I do. You would follow so closely that I was constantly stumbling over you. I wonder what you thought about those countless, sweet times. Surely you had more interesting things to do than to stand guard, leaning into me for hours on end. And, your quiet loyalty touched me in a special way.

Do you remember? Of course you do. Your memories etched the responses for the rhythm of your days. Your life was not over-burdened by the human dilemma. It was simple and focused. And we were the beneficiaries of your perspective.

Your blind eyes. We speculate you must have bumped into something or stumbled the night your legs quit working. A disk high in your spine was completely displaced.

You could not stand, and were too weary to do more than lay your head on my hand as we took you to the vet. When I called the next morning and was told there was no hope, I said we would be in to see you. I called your girls, away at college now, to tell them the sad news. I am glad they were spared this painful goodbye. For you, though, I would have wished you could have been wrapped in their love one last time.

We raced over to see you, unable to present the cheery front we wanted. It was cruel to have to make such a decision for you. Pumped full of medicines, and unable to stand, you talked your joy at seeing us. You told us how bad it had been, how happy you were we were taking you out of that place. We had a wonderful conversation. You knew we loved you, you knew we were there, you knew we thought you were a "good girl"—your most prized words. Your cry when we left ripped through us both.

So, Monty, we laid you under the junipers, your collar high in the trees. You looked so much like our sleeping little dog it was hard to believe you were past sleeping. You earned a place in our hearts with your persistence, enthusiasm, and love. You will always be a member of our family—part and parcel of our precious memories. You were our friend.

We are a "cat" family. Now, we are also a "dog" family.

There will not be another dog for awhile. We could never have another terrier-mix. That is our weakness, Monty, and our understanding there could never be another like you. But, our tribute to you is we want another dog in our lives—someday.

Rest well, Monty.

Betti Bernardi

Help Wanted: Canine Caretaker

You can say any fool thing to a dog, and the dog will give you this look that says, "My God, you're right! I never would've thought of that!"

Dave Barry

EDITOR'S NOTE: *This is yet another atypical dog story. We've included it because it highlights the joys—and the less joyful aspects—of owning a dog. Or, perhaps we should say, being owned by a dog.*

Staff person wanted for an elderly, nervous dachshund. Several skills are needed to meet the demands of the job.

Applicants must be alert and proactive. Nervous dogs often barf (yes, barf, not bark) with only a split-second notice. Alert assistants will have quick reflexes and the strength to scoop up the hound and head for the nearest non-textile floor covering. The most proactive interested parties will have scoped out all such floor coverings and know the quickest routes to them.

Adept companions will have a bucket, cleaning cloths, and enzyme eating Barf-b-Gone organized and available at all times. Experienced applicants will know where to get the gallon-sized jugs at the cheapest cost.

Since the position requires applicants to live-in, smart prospects will not allow the dog to sleep in bed with them, but right next to the bed where an eye and ear can be constantly on watch. There is no sleeping on the job. Breaks are few and far-between, usually taken while the nervous-bellied one rests quietly on your lap.

By far the most important quality for the successful candidate will be dedication and a caring attitude. Blind loyalty doesn't hurt. Without these traits, it is difficult to manage the job. To get up in the wee hours of the morning to attend to the distressed canine and clean up after a nauseating episode is not easy. To have the persistence to get stains out of car seats and carpeting and make continual efforts to deodorize vehicles is a thankless, never-ending job.

A good caretaker will not care what other people think, as episodes will occur in front of friends and family as well as strangers. Most episodes will happen at the most inopportune of times such as at the last minute you can leave for an appointment without being late or when the house is being shown to a prospective buyer.

Only those who will be a loving parent to this pet need apply. There is no pay. The winning applicant will be required to meet all expenses, including food, medical care, and the necessary cleaning supplies.

There are only perks to this position. A fuzzy face that will always be happy to see you will constantly follow you around and look at you with adoring eyes. A warm little body will curl up next to you and keep you toasty warm on the couch. Your companion will issue no criticisms or judge you in light of your weight, race, gender, or hygiene. Best of all, hounds usually agree with everything you say.

Elaine Whitesides

Dog is My Co-Pilot

You learn in this business: If you want a friend, get a dog.
Carl Icahn, US auto business executive

Max, the Belgian sheepdog, was my right-hand dog. I was working as a dog groomer in central Illinois. I had a twenty-four-foot recreational vehicle kitted out as a grooming shop with all the amenities. Max rode with me on many of my appointments. By the time he was eight years old, he would sit quietly in the driver's seat or on the central hump between the seats called a doghouse. He never bothered any of my clients or their masters. Often they wouldn't even notice he was there. We had spent several years in obedience classes and practicing the skills required to work together seamlessly.

He was never aggressive with the younger dogs in our house. We had two younger female Belgian sheepdogs who would grab his neck or ear in their teeth and attempt to haul him about. He would put up with it for a while, but in the end, he would just disengage without a sound and go lie under the kitchen table where the puppies couldn't get as good a hold on him.

On weekends, Max and I would go camping at local campgrounds. One summer, we decided to go to a large event in western Pennsylvania. This was the longest trip we had taken in the recreational vehicle, but with a handful of dog food and ten gallons of water we set off to the event. Several of my friends wanted to go along, and since there was lots of room, we let them come. We left central Illinois at 4 p.m., intending to get into the campground at about 7 a.m. the next day.

I really didn't trust anybody else to drive the recreational vehicle, as it takes a bit of getting used to when all you have ever driven is subcompact cars. My passengers assured me they would keep me amused and awake for the whole drive. By the time we hit the Indiana line, four of my passengers were sleeping in the back seats of the recreational vehicle, and my navigator was nodding off in the right-hand captain's chair. Max was also dozing, curled up on the doghouse.

We stopped for gas and a stretch just past Indianapolis, and all of my human passengers resumed their slumber. Sometime around 3:30 a.m., I started getting sleepy as well, and that was when I noticed Max was wide awake and alert. He put his head in my lap and looked up at me, as if to say, "Wouldn't you like to take a break, and walk the nice dog?"

I pulled off in the middle of that empty stretch of highway and walked about with Max. Then I filled up his water dish and we walked about some more. It was probably the most critical fifteen minutes of the drive that night. I started to feel more lively and awake, so we got back in the recreational vehicle and finished the drive with no more drowsiness. Max did not sleep either.

For the rest of the drive, he stayed with me and together we completed the ride. When we pulled into the campground, the other humans in the recreational vehicle started to wake up. They never knew how close I had come to driving off into a ditch or that Max had taken control of the situation to avoid that happening.

That is a heroic dog.

Wolf Halton

Doggone It, I'm in Love Again

Dogs are wise agents, sent directly from heaven.
Susan Ariel Rainbow Kennedy

Imagine my dismay when my 18-year-old son arrived home recently with a pretty girl slung over his shoulder.

Said he met her through a friend of a friend. It only cost him $100 to bring her home.

Black hair, brown eyes, big butt, bad breath, and a brindled tail whipping around like a plane propeller.

"I'm going to call her Kirra. You know, the surfboard company," he announced, dropping ten pounds of puppy onto the just-cleaned kitchen floor.

"Oh God!"

"Yeah, she's a pit bull, Mom. But don't freak. I saw her parents. They're great. None of the stuff they say in the newspaper is true."

"Are you sure - *none* of it?"

Surfboard puppy was pulling at my sneaker laces and nipping at the tip of the shoe. She stopped just long enough to catch my eye. And then pee at my feet.

And so it was I met my new best pal, one of seven pit bull puppies born weeks ago in a Lower Makefield farmhouse.

The one who wants to chase balls, but not return them, and snuggle in my lap in the morning, making it hard to read the paper and juggle my coffee. The one who licks my face with pure joy no matter how many times I tell her to knock it off because it's soooo disgusting.

I've heard all the bad stuff about this breed, so I gathered all the info I could on the oft-maligned American pit bull terrier, a World War I soldier dog known for its courage, strength, tenacity, and locking jaw. *Locking jaw?*

Characteristics that made it attractive to dog fighters and thugs looking for a macho pooch.

Not to worry, say breed experts. If we spend lots of quality time with Kirra and train her with love and patience and a firm hand, she'll grow to be a sweet and loyal pet.

If we don't, will she eat us in our sleep?

That's what my husband predicts will happen. I'm thinking she'll eat him first, since I'm the one who buys the chew toys. The commotion should give me enough time to lock myself in the master bathroom and call animal control.

She seemed too little to eat us on her first night at home. So I let her conk out on top of me on the family room couch, her head nuzzled under my chin and the rest spread out over my chest like dead weight.

Very endearing once I got used to the puffs of puppy breath and the intermittent snoring.

"You're kidding, right?" my husband asked when I told him I wouldn't be coming up to bed.

"The books say to take her outdoors every hour. Joe wanted to put her in his bed, but he has school in the morning. No way he can be up all night. I'm close to the back door here."

And so it was I saw 1 a.m. and 3 a.m. and 4:30 a.m. all of that first week and into the second.

It wasn't so bad. I was freezing cold, a little sleep-deprived, but who knew the sky was so pretty or the busy neighborhood so still right before dawn? Still—except for me, dressed in flannel pajamas and a long dress coat chasing an escaped puppy through the pine trees.

"She's a flight risk. We need a fence," I told my husband in the morning.

"We need our heads examined," he answered.

But I'm thinking maybe the hassle will be worth it.

This little poop machine could be a bridge to my kid.

It's not easy to talk to an 18-year-old boy. Especially not if you are his busybody mom and you haven't a clue about sports, cars, motorcycles, surfing, fishing, extreme skating, or the new "Boys Set Fire" CD.

With Kirra, we finally had something to talk about again.

We even went shopping together. Chose a crate and chew toys. Debated the best puppy chow. Argued about the spike collar he insisted on. I liked the hot purple nylon ditty.

"She's a pit bull, Mom, not some sissy dog."

He's going to help his dad fence the yard, and in the meantime he's teaching me to whistle for her instead of chasing across the lawns. And he's the one who told me it's a bad idea to keep bathing her. "You're drying her out! Dogs are supposed to stink."

And while it's not nearly as important as reconnecting to my boy, I'm also reconnecting with the neighborhood.

Mr. Brophy and his chocolate Lab have lived down the street for years. We talked for the first time this week when Kirra made the Lab's acquaintance as Brophy and I navigated the icy sidewalk one morning before work.

And one night I finally met the lady who walks that old, gentle-faced dog. Turns out she's a dog trainer. Gave me some tips on a good puppy school.

I also got some advice from my next-door neighbor, a guy with a big but very polite German shepherd named Max.

Mr. Kim on the other side came over to meet Kirra, too. He doesn't have a dog. And I don't think he's real keen on them, but he gave her a pat and a cheerful smile anyway. So she doesn't eat him, I guess.

Same with the propane delivery guy. He left a dog treat along with my bill.

And Annie, the little girl across the street, carried her dog over one day. I thought Kirra would lose her Milk-Bone®-addled mind when Annie opened up that bowling bag and Belle, a fat little Chihuahua, popped straight out.

All of a sudden, I'm having more fun, and I have a pint-sized pit bull to thank for it.

Be sure to call and remind me I said that when you read she's eaten my husband in his sleep.

Kate Fratti

My Little Diplomat

My little dog—a heartbeat at my feet.

Edith Wharton

Nathaniel was the first dog that was entirely my responsibility. I was twenty-one when I left home and found myself living next door to a couple who had a cute little poodle with a litter of pups. They suspected a terrier living in the next block had fathered her brood.

Barely six weeks old when I brought him home, he was a cute little guy, but as he grew, he got uglier by the day. His coat stuck out in every direction like a bottle brush and was black, flecked with gray; not the most attractive of color combinations. He was slim with legs way too long for his body and his goofy-looking tail curled in an arch over his back. Literally everyone who saw him teased me about what a ridiculous-looking little animal he was. Yet, in the end, he always won their hearts. He was Mr. Personality; a homely little dog that made friends everywhere we went.

When I got him, I was just entering my hippie phase. I moved around a lot, switched boyfriends fairly often, hitchhiked when my junk-heap of a car wasn't running, and generally lived a lifestyle most dogs would have found difficult to accept. Not Nathaniel. I could take him anywhere and as soon as he inspected the place a bit, he would settle in with ease. Even without a leash, he never ran into the street, or made messes inside; and he learned to sit up and beg, which increased his appeal to everyone we encountered during our adventures. He was the perfect traveling companion and his manners were impeccable. Somehow, he always seemed to know just how to act in every situation.

He did get lost once. He followed my girlfriend's Irish setter when she dug under the fence to escape in search of a doggie adventure. Nathaniel was unfamiliar with the area and apparently, couldn't keep up with the bigger dog or find his way back. I was fearful and worried

31

when the setter came home without him. He was wearing a nametag, but he was so ugly, I was afraid no one would bother to help him.

He not only found a sympathetic soul who called me, but when I went to get him, I discovered she lived in one of the most affluent neighborhoods I had ever seen. I passed one mansion after another until I came to the address. There were iron gates and an intercom that I buzzed, even as I wondered if this could really be the right house. Sure enough, the gates parted and a voice told me to drive on in.

As I approached the house, the front door opened and there stood a woman with a cute little Yorkshire terrier under one arm and Nathaniel under the other. She told me if he hadn't had the nametag she would have kept him because, other than her little Yorkie, he was the sweetest and smartest dog she had ever encountered. To get her attention, he walked up to her in a parking lot, barked, then twirled on his hind legs before coming to rest in his "sit up and beg" position.

"It was as if he was asking me to read his tag," she gushed, as she handed him to me.

Being beautiful can be a great advantage, but Nathaniel taught me what's on the inside is infinitely more powerful and important than what's on the outside. Whenever I'm feeling insecure because of a bad hair day or a few extra pounds I can't seem to lose, I remember my homely little dog who managed to get positive feedback from everyone he ever met.

A couple of years ago I ran into a guy I hadn't seen for almost three decades. Within two minutes he brought up the ugly little dog he remembered was always with me and asked whatever happened to him. I told him Nathaniel had lived almost seventeen years; longer than any other dog I've ever owned.

"He sure was something," my friend commented.

He was right.

Susanne Fogle

A Good Deed Dog

He is your friend, your partner, your defender, your dog. You are his life, his love, his leader. He will be yours, faithful and true, to the last beat of his heart. You owe it to him to be worthy of such devotion.

Unknown

As the beautiful Current River winds its way through our county, it sings its sometimes tumultuous, sometimes placid song. The blue-green waters of the river are home to many species of fish, and on its banks and in the sky above it, wildlife thrives.

Should one be fishing on the river in the fall of the year, one is likely to see an osprey dive in, just ahead, and come up with a fish in his talons. The great blue heron is a patron of the river year- round, and bald eagles soar the skies here in the winter.

People from all across the country come to enjoy the Current River. Fishing, boating, swimming, camping, and inner tubing are all popular activities. But my favorite thing to do on the river is to go out on the jet-ski, courtesy of my son, Greg, drive up several miles, shut the motor off, and allow the currents of the river to carry us back at a leisurely pace. It is a totally relaxing floating experience with much to see and ruminate upon. Gazing down into the clear water, I'm likely to see a river bass swim by. Gazing into the sky, a red-tailed hawk might be soaring gracefully. And on the shores, I have seen a wild turkey hen having a drink with her turkey chicks. Beauty, serenity, and cool breezes make for a most pleasant experience on these excursions.

Sometimes, though, a boat ride may net an unexpected surprise. Such as the one we had on a lovely fall day a few years ago. Greg had just shut the motor off, and I leaned back and let one of my feet dangle in the cool water. The trees on the bluffs above the river were dressed in their fall finery, the sky was exceptionally blue, and some turtles were taking a sun bath on a fallen tree branch in the water.

Suddenly, the peace and tranquility of the moment were interrupted by the piercing, pitiful cries of an animal.

"Greg, an animal is in distress up ahead. Let's go see what it is," I immediately suggested. Of course, Greg, having inherited a soft spot for helpless animals from his mom, did exactly what I asked.

"Oh, look, there is something on that gravel bar," I cried, as we approached the small gravel island surrounded on all sides by water. "It's a tiny puppy, Greg. Someone has abandoned that poor little animal right there on the gravel bar!"

"Well, they probably knew you'd be out on the river today, Mom," my son remarked, as he maneuvered the boat to the gravel bar. I jumped into the shallow water and rushed to the crying, black puppy, scooping it up into my arms. The puppy whimpered as I got back into the boat with it.

"It's a little female, and she is covered with some sort of grease," I said, as it rubbed off all over me. "The stuff smells like motor oil. Now why would someone douse this puppy with motor oil?"

The puppy whimpered again, then settled into my lap quietly, while I kept stroking its greasy back the rest of the way home.

As it turned out, the little foundling was infested with fleas, so a thorough bath and health check were in order.

"It's part Lab, part who-knows-what," the vet said the following day. "But she seems to be in good health." After her puppy shots, I took the foundling home, where she would join my animal menagerie. A couple of months later, she went back and got spayed, as well.

I named the puppy Blackie, but call her Yuppie, and she turned out to be the most faithful, watchful, and loving companion anyone could ask for. A couple of years later, Yuppie repaid my good deed with a good deed of her own.

We were walking in the woods together one spring morning, as we often do, for we love the woods, when I stepped over a fallen log. The next thing I knew Yuppie had rushed to my side and grabbed hold of something. It was a copperhead snake that was about to grab hold on my foot! I shrieked and ran from the area, and soon Yuppie was right behind me. When we got back to the yard, I was about to properly thank her for saving me from a venomous snakebite, when I noticed her head was already swelling. She had been bitten right on the side of her head!

Of course, I called the vet, but he reassured me dogs, unlike humans, recover from a venomous snakebite on their own. All I could do was to make her as comfortable as possible, while she laid around for a week with her head and body swelled three times their normal size. And I did just that, and soon she was back to her normal, playful self.

But I found out later they do have an anti-venom serum for dogs and cats, and Yuppie was lucky to survive without help. Had I known about it right away, I would have taken my faithful friend for that shot, and it would have, no doubt, cut down on the misery she was feeling for several days.

I have always believed good deeds get their just reward in the end. Of course, Blackie, my faithful, loving companion for ten years now, has proven that many times.

Renie Burghardt

Hans Was Here

You think dogs will not be in heaven? I tell you, they will be there long before any of us.

Robert Louis Stevenson

In March 1992, some close family members in California gave my sister and brother-in-law, Christine and Dick, a miniature schnauzer puppy. Dick and Christine named him Hans, and we all fell head-over-heels in love with the cute little guy.

In January 2005, I was spending some time after the Christmas holidays with Christine and Dick at their home in Webster, New York. Hans was now aging, but still not terribly old for a miniature schnauzer.

He'd been having some minor physical problems. Or at least we thought they were minor. So Christine made an appointment with Hans' veterinarian for minor surgery. On a cold grey January morning, she and I took him in for his appointment. He was always nervous when he knew he was going to the vet's office. As soon as we got into the office, he made a beeline for the door. "Let me out of here!" is what I'm sure was going through his little mind.

Ever since he'd been a puppy thirteen years earlier, Hans never liked to be held. He was loving and affectionate, but was definitely not a "lap dog." He was so scared that morning at the vet's office, I just instinctively picked him up while Christine was filling out the paperwork. He snuggled close to me, burrowing into my heavy winter coat. In all his life, he'd never allowed me to hold him.

That was the first and last time it ever happened.

Later that day, while Christine, Dick, and I were having lunch, the phone rang. Christine answered the call, and then started sobbing. It was the vet. Dick and I knew without knowing—Hans was gone. The surgery was normally minor, but Hans' heart stopped in the middle of it. And they could not revive him.

Later that afternoon, the three of us went to the vet's office to pay our final respects to this beloved little creature who had become as precious to us as our children.

The staff ladies had Hans laid out on a table in one of the back rooms. He looked so peaceful and beautiful. Christine, Dick, and I said our separate goodbyes to Hans.

When my turn came, I bent over his body, laid my hand on his head, and kissed him. "Goodbye, Hans," was all I could say. Then, tears streaming down my face, I glanced at him one last time, and walked out.

The ride home was silent. The day was cold and grey, and matched our mood.

That night at dinner, we drank a toast to our beloved Hans.

On the following October 15, Dick died. He'd been ailing for years with a lung disease, and his death was not unexpected. So I made the long sad journey back to New York from my home in Wyoming. I spent nearly three months there with Christine and the rest of our family, doing what I could to help her through her own difficult transition.

Two days before I went back home to Wyoming, I awoke at 4:30 the morning of January 10. As I lay there, deciding whether to get up or go back to sleep, I heard a car door slam at a nearby neighbor's house. Then I heard Hans' loud, familiar bark in the living room directly below my bedroom.

Oh well, I thought, he's just barking because he also heard the car door slam.

Then I did a mental double-take. It was almost exactly a year ago, on January 17, 2005, Hans had died! The memory of that day is permanently etched on my memory.

But I knew his bark, and I felt his energy in the house. What was going on here?

The next morning, I said to Christine, "Something strange happened last night. Hans was here."

I spent quite a bit of time thinking about all that had happened. I believe our animal family live beyond the veil of death, just as we humans do. And I believe those who love us, human or animal, never leave us. They often have a desire, from beyond the grave, to help us and to let us know they are still alive, still loving us.

A week or so after Hans died, I received a message I can only describe as coming from the world of spirit. Here it is:

> If there is one *major* lesson your pets have to teach you, it is this: *Live in the moment!* And this: *Love unconditionally.*
>
> Your pets find joy, passion, and pleasure in every moment of their physical lives. Even when they appear to you to be suffering from some physical illness or injury.
>
> Pets—and all animals, in fact—have no fear of illness or death. And, more importantly, they have no fear of life. Hence they immerse themselves in all the pleasures of physical existence. And they do it without hesitation and without guilt.
>
> They are fully alive in every moment. Not a bad role model for you to follow!
>
> Animals do not live with the same "agendas" you humans do. They have no desire to control or manipulate their fellow creatures, human or animal. Their intent is to simply live freely and joyously. They see little difference between life and death.
>
> No matter how awful (or peaceful) their transition from life to death appears to you, those transitions are always easy and effortless to them.
>
> And when they arrive "on the other side," they continue their joyful, exuberant, and happy lives, romping and playing with abandon.
>
> They often return to visit you. As do your human loved ones. But most of you are not open, at least not fully open, to that happening for you. When you do not believe, you cannot see. You often say, "When I see it, I'll believe it." But it's always the other way around—when you believe it, you'll see it.

You never lose those you love. If you remain open to them, "alive" or "dead," you will always be comforted by them. You will feel their presence, their energy.

And you will know you are loved.

Hans really was here. Visiting from heaven, I suppose.

John Cali

Shared Angst

Dogs love company. They place it first on their short list of needs.

J.R. Ackerley

I pulled out the suitcase and began packing for another three-day excursion to the house we recently purchased four hours south. As I pulled underwear and socks out of drawers I noticed Simon peaking around the corner at me. Simon is my fourteen-year old deaf dachshund who is, shall we just politely say, a little quirky. I've had five dachshunds in the last forty years and he is by far the one with the most issues.

I'm not saying Simon is as bad as Pete, the dachshund of a friend of mine. Pete's owner travels about 150 days out of each year and Pete does not like being left behind. When my friend takes out his suitcase he has to really watch his dachshund. Pete has the habit of relieving himself in the bag—but only after it has been packed. There's nothing like a little surprise when you get to some hotel far from home. No, Simon is not like that.

Simon just gets really nervous. When the house is getting cleaned and furniture is being moved, he just gets anxious—and throws up. Or when he doesn't eat on schedule, his stomach must churn—and he throws up. Or when people come and he doesn't warm to them right away, he hides—and he throws up. Or when he isn't getting enough attention—even that seems to make him throw up. He is obviously a dog who needs a routine, a schedule to live through each day without variance so he stays on an even keel. No surprises—just the same old thing day in and day out. I think that would make him happiest.

But our life just isn't like that, especially in the last eight months. We've been traveling between two homes in two states. Simon and I have not been in one place longer than two weeks at a time. I fret and worry and try to be proactive by always having the cleaning cloths and enzyme-eating cleaning solution handy. I try to keep him fed and watered on a somewhat timely basis. But I just expect I will be

40

cleaning up and washing blankets and rugs all the time; so I just leave a bucket in the car with all the supplies.

Today when I started packing my bag and noticed Simon peaking, I just set down my clothes and went to look for him—and his barf. All in a day's routine for us. But I didn't find any. In fact, I met Simon in the hallway. He was coming back toward the bedroom with the corner of his pink, queen-sized blanket in his mouth. He dragged it right by me and into the bedroom where he stopped at the edge of the bed next to my suitcase. He started fluffing and circling and finally curled up into a ball on it.

Watching him calmly sleep I realized the change in him. He wasn't pacing. I realized I hadn't needed to clean up any barf for some time. I sat down on the floor next to him and touched his head. He startled as he usually does since he can't hear. But then he adjusted his position so he was leaning next to me and put his head on my thigh. While I rubbed his ear he closed his eyes and began snoring.

I wondered how long it had been since he was the dog who paced and threw up when I packed. I remembered the last few times we traveled he would wait by the door and be the first one out and into the car. He would even sit in the car and watch me load. I kind of laughed because I always worried about having a dog out without a leash. Now I realized that car wasn't going anywhere without him. His blanket would be piled up on the passenger seat in front and in the five minutes it took to get on the highway, he would have burrowed into it and be into the third chorus of snoring. I couldn't remember the last time he had thrown up in the car. We'd been in such a state of constant motion I hadn't considered the adjustments we'd all made in our personal habits.

So I patted his head and got up to finish packing. I gathered his harness, leash, dishes, and food into the usual tote bag and set it next to his blanket. He looked up at me and sniffed the air toward the bag. He sat watching as I finished gathering toiletries and zipped up my suitcase. I pulled up the handle and slipped the straps of his bag of goodies over it, wheeling everything out of the bedroom and next to the front door. Simon grabbed a mouthful of blanket and followed me. He knew he was coming, too and that apparently made everything just fine with him.

I guess in the whole scheme of things, it is inevitable that times and people and places change. It is wonderful to know my old dog *can* learn new tricks in the face of all this change and relieve his angst all on his own. For this I am thankful. But I think I'll still check to make sure that bucket is in the trunk of the car.

Elaine Whitesides

A Painted Pony for Fitzgerald

What dogs? These are my children, little people with fur who make my heart open a little wider.

Oprah Winfrey

Be honest—dogs love toys. I don't know if that's because most of us assume our first purchase of puppy chow must also include a toy purchase. You would think dog food companies would put doggie toys in puppy chow bags the way cereal makers did for us when we were kids. Whether dogs are conditioned to love toys, or it is innate behavior, remains to be seen.

Now, there are two types of dogs when it comes to toys. The first kind loves its toys at first, chews them up, rolls them under the sofa (and forgets about them), or just plain loses interest in its playthings altogether. Many dogs outgrow toys. For whatever reason, I don't know.

The second category of dog is what I refer to as a bona fide "toy-dog." It's the real McCoy. These dogs are easily recognizable. They strategically position their toys in places like the doorway to the bathroom, the hallway, or in any frequently traveled pathway in the house. They love to hoard their toys, pile them into stacks, then fetch one at a time to play with, and perhaps return the toy to the pile (not likely!). If you miss stepping on the thing, yet toss it out of the way, which indicates you want to play with it, then count on the pup bringing you the toy and offering to "share" it with you. Toy-dogs are always eager to share.

You might have read elsewhere[7] our dogs have always celebrated Christmas gift-giving with us. On all occasions there has been a toy (or two) along with a treat to eat waiting for our dogs under the tree. This past Christmas was our miniature schnauzer Fitzgerald's first Christmas, and this year was no different from any previous year.

---

[7] See the chapter, "The Happiest Dog at Christmas."

43

Who says you must buy your dog toys at a pet store? When I want to buy toys, I go to a toy store. I'm not plugging Toys "R" Us, but let's face it, it's a fabulous store. I knew I'd find something special for Fitzgerald and, sure enough, a huge (at least twice his size) stuffed pinto pony, what many folks call the "painted pony," sat on the shelf begging to go home with me.

When I reached checkout, it was packed. Cashiers were opening additional registers as fast as shoppers showed up. Somehow I got at the head of a new line with my single-item purchase. A fellow looking like he was buying something for a niece stepped in behind me with a single-item purchase as well.

He looked around at the other customers with their overflowing carts, and then at me and said, "Seems like we're the only ones buying just one thing." He added, "I only have one niece, for now." I'm not sure if he meant that as an apology or what.

So I said to him, "I only have one dog and this is his big present."

I'm relatively sure I didn't raise my voice and, in fact, I spoke as softly as I would have in a quiet room. Yet, everyone nearby must have heard me, for what followed was a collective "Gasp!" They say seeing is believing and I'm absolutely positive I saw the haughty stares from other shoppers squinting at me like I had committed the most heinous sacrilege in the world. I speculated some folks were strapped for cash and had made great sacrifices to pay for those heaped-up carts of toys and, in some cases, two heaped-up carts. Maybe they thought I was putting on the Ritz buying my pup a painted pony, but that was not the case. I merely wanted Fitzgerald to have a nice toy. After all, I was certain he was a genuine toy-dog and he would have to appreciate such a fine addition to his array of playthings.

When I arrived home, my wife asked me why I had purchased such a large pony.

"Fitzgerald loves to wallow and this will be the perfect thing for him to wallow with," I said.

We agreed this present might suit him well. Also, we agreed his pony would be the one toy that was off-limits to us in order to prevent him from becoming too rough with it and shredding it to pieces. So far, that has worked. And it goes without saying Fitzgerald loves his pony.

At times when I observe the happy face sewn onto the pony's head, I pretend it has a personality. I imagine when Fitzgerald is slinging it around it might say, "Oh no, how did this happen to me? I thought I was destined for a human toddler cuddling with me."

At other times, I envision a very serene countenance upon the pony's face, especially when I walk into the room and discover Fitzgerald sleeping on the floor snuggled close to his pony with his front leg thrown over it. Fitzgerald also wears a serene face. When I recall the collective gasp I heard from the shoppers in Toys "R" Us at Christmastime, I remember a line from an old movie I once saw: "Aw heck, every kid ought to have a pony."

Robert Paul Blumenstein

My Dog Thinks I'm a Sheep (Is That Baaad?)

My dog is usually pleased with what I do, because she is not infected with the concept of what I "should" be doing.

Lonzo Idolswine

My husband and I wanted a great Pyrenees because they're known for being a gentle, devoted breed that is good with children. Okay, that and because they're big, white, and fluffy. When we saw a breeder a mere two hours' drive from our home had great Pyrenees puppies, we were there. (Also, it was winter and we had to get our two children out of the house before they killed each other. We figured a four-hour road trip would allow us all to live to see another day.)

We arrived at the farm where we were taken through the sheep pasture to the barn. The pups' mother had been removed to a stall near the back of the barn as she was very protective of her litter. I gleefully pushed past my children, held out my arms and gathered as many of the cottony, tail-wagging, tongue-lapping fluff balls to me as I could. There were seven pups, and three or four squirmed into my embrace as the others waddled off to investigate my husband and children. We were in love. All of us. Me, the puppies, the children, even the husband. And so Robyn (so named because my four-year-old son *is* Batman) became a part of our family.

Much like in *Clifford The Small Red Puppy* (a book by Norman Bridwell), Robyn grew and grew and *grew*. I recently learned how protective Robyn has become when a neighbor's Rottweiler came over to visit. He and Robyn were playing happily. I've known Vader (yes, as in Darth) since he was a pup, so I went out to say hello. When I reached out to give Vader a scratch behind the ears, Robyn lurched between us and gave Vader a menacing growl. I went back inside.

While a door-to-door salesman was canvassing our neighborhood, I sat in our swing enjoying the warmth of the day. Robyn leapt into the swing and lay across my lap until the man went away. Needless to say, I didn't even have to say, "No, thank you, we're not interested."

I was flattered but a little perplexed by this behavior until I was leafing through a friend's dog training book. In this particular book, various breeds of dogs were listed. Naturally, I looked up great Pyrenees so I could puff out my chest and be reassured I'm the proud owner of not only a fabulous dog, but of a dog that is a member of a fabulous breed. The book confirmed the great Pyrenees is intelligent and devoted. It warned, however, you must be firm in showing this breed you are in charge because if it perceives you to be weak and incapable of defending yourself—that is, a sheep—it will be protective and possibly aggressive.

I looked at my friend. "Robyn thinks I'm a sheep," I said. "Do you think we should take an obedience class?"

I mentioned to my husband that perhaps Robyn and I should take a class, though I must admit, I'm reluctant to do so. Is it really such a bad thing that my dog sees me as a lash-fluttering, defenseless female when to the rest of the world I must try to appear as a superwoman who juggles to balance work and family? Is it so terrible while I'm counting calories, my faithful companion sees me not as fat, but fluffy? So what if the white knight that comes to my rescue slobbers, sheds, and snorts? Some gals don't have a knight at all.

So I ask you if my dog thinks I'm a sheep, is that bad?

Naaaaa.

Gayle Trent

Rocky on Guard

If your dog doesn't like someone you probably shouldn't either.

Unknown

Rocky was a large, powerfully built Alaskan malamute. His muscular body was broad and strong, and he was tall enough to put his front paws on my shoulders when he stood on his hind feet. He had coarse, thick hair that begged you to run your fingers through it, and short pointed ears that were silky soft to the touch. Silver and black with touches of cream, he was a beautiful animal who enjoyed howling at the moon on dark, starlit nights. His voice created an eerie, mournful music that made the hairs on my arms stand up whenever I heard him.

An avowed outside dog, the big husky hated to come in the house and I could usually get him inside only after bribing him with chunks of his favorite food. As soon as he finished his treat, he was ready to go right back outside. No matter what I tried, I just couldn't convince him it would be fun to be a house dog.

One Friday evening, my husband left for an out-of-town weekend business trip. With only Laura, my two-year-old daughter, and Rocky for company, I looked forward to spending a couple of quiet days catching up on my reading. To my surprise, just before dark that night Rocky began whining and pawing at the front door. There was no mistaking his meaning. He wanted in! Puzzled, I held the door open and he sauntered inside like he owned the place.

With one swish of his bushy tail, he swept everything off the coffee table. Laura giggled in delight as I pretended to scold him. Rocky curled his upper lip to grin at me and strolled away to investigate the rest of the house, Laura tagging along behind him. Before long, the two settled in her room, where Rocky decided to lie in the doorway. His shaggy body filled up the narrow space, and he gave no indication he wanted to go back outside.

Before long, it was Laura's bedtime. As she drifted off to sleep, the dog curled in a tight ball and dozed off, too. I got myself a snack and a magazine, and settled in to read. The house was so quiet, I forgot all about Rocky.

Sometime later, a loud vehicle drove up in front of the house. Somebody turning around, I thought. Then the engine shut off and a door slammed. I hurried to the window and peeked out between the miniblind slats. A scruffy-looking young man was stepping onto the porch.

He looked vaguely familiar, like someone I might have met before. Cautiously, I opened the heavy wooden door a crack. The man pulled the outer storm door open and propped against it.

"Hi," he said. His tone was friendly but the icy look in his eyes sent a warning chill rippling up my spine. "I heard your husband was out of town for the weekend and I thought I'd check on you."

Alarm bells clanged in my brain. In the space of a second, the horrible thought I had to get rid of this man or both my daughter and I would be in serious danger, raged through my mind.

"I'm fine," I replied as firmly as I could. My mouth felt like it was full of sawdust. "There's really no need for you to be concerned. Thanks for stopping."

I reached for the storm door but he jerked it open wider and parked one foot on the threshold. My heart crammed itself painfully into my throat.

"I think I'll visit for a little while," he said, and started to step into the living room. Terrified, I tried to shove the heavy wooden door shut but he blocked it and forced it open, pushing me back into the room.

Suddenly, the man froze, his eyes riveted on something behind me. I glanced around and there stood Rocky, his lovely plumed tail waving gently back and forth. His lips curled back in a huge nasty smile that exposed every sharp, wicked-looking tooth in his head. My knees went weak.

"D-does that dog bite?" the man stammered.

"Yes," I said. "He sure does."

"Sorry to have bothered you." The man abruptly let go of the door and stumbled backwards, his eyes fixed on Rocky. I slammed the door shut and turned the locks. A few seconds later, the truck engine roared to life and sped away.

Trembling, I dropped to the floor and threw my arms around Rocky's neck, burying my face in his beautiful fur. He panted cheerfully as I hugged and kissed him and told him what a wonderful boy he was. There was no doubt in my mind he had saved Laura and me from something too horrible to think about.

As if he sensed the danger had passed, Rocky asked to go outside. Overwhelmed with emotion, I watched him romp around the moonlit yard. How had he known we would need his protection? Why did he pick this particular night to ask to come in the house? After a few moments, I decided not to question his knowledge. Instead, I whispered a few heartfelt prayers of thanks for Rocky's wisdom and courage.

Anne C. Watkins

Nest Empty Except for Superdog

You do not own a dog, the dog owns you.

Unknown

Readers tell me I am not the only empty nester whose kids have left behind scrapbooks, dusty collections, Beastie Boy band posters, and the dog they promised to take with them. There ought to be some kind of law to prohibit this kind of dumping, especially the doggy kind.

A kid's other stuff can be packed away in the attic. A kid's best friend—in this case, sixty pounds of boundless energy, muddy snoot and pleading, gentle brown eyes—is another story.

Trust me. Two toddlers were a cakewalk compared to this. It might look like I'm rubbing the pup's belly, but really I'm looking for an off switch.

I no sooner reach the kitchen to fumble for coffee and some breakfast each morning when my brindle-colored pal is dancing and tail-wagging in anticipation of a new day.

"Whoa! Finally! You're up! I thought you were dead. Let's play! C'mon, what'll it be? Ball? Tug a dish towel? You chase me, then I chase you? Ma, we're gonna play now, right? What's that you're making? Toast? I *love* toast! I do! I really, really do!"

If I had a quarter of this animal's energy and zest for life, I'd conquer the world. Or at least organize the linen closet and vacuum the upstairs. When I try, she steals the washcloths and chases the vacuum cleaner.

"Please. Take her to work with you," I begged my husband as the pup, a year-old American Staffordshire terrier pushed at the back of my legs with the remains of an "indestructible" ball she'd chewed into a half sphere.

"Ma, remember this toy? Remember? It's fun, really fun! Do you mind if I lick your knees?"

My son, the dog dumper, sometimes could be counted on to walk the Energizer Pup. Before he left, he pointed out a winding woodland trail where he liked to run her.

"She loves the woods, Mom. It'll be fun for you, too."

Fun is a strong word. But the trails beat an endless, slobbery tennis ball toss, and I often can convince the dumper's dad to come along.

Both of us agree we are way too old and out of shape for climbing ridges, balancing on log bridges, and slogging through thickets to keep up with a four-legged dynamo. We do it anyway, just to poop her out. We're the ones who need the nap afterward.

On the trail, the pooch circles back on occasion like Lassie to be sure we're keeping up. She looks sympathetic, but a little disappointed, when one of us plunks down on a fallen tree to catch a breath.

"What's the matter? Oh, you're OK. You are! Let's go! Let's go! C'mon, I saw a squirrel! You see the squirrel? Hey! Look, I'm wearing your scarf! You like it when I stick my tongue in your ear, don't you, Ma? Here, I'll wet the other one."

"You have to tell her who's boss," a more experienced dog owner advised me when I complained.

"I'm boss," I told the pup very firmly the very next day.

"I know you're boss, Ma! I know! You pick the game, Boss! C'mon! Hurry! Ooops! Sorry, Boss. Me bad. I forgot—no jumping!"

If there was a time I worried I would be bored and lonesome without children to care for, that time has passed. Today, I am completely at the mercy of a new creature—one who, unlike kids, shows no signs of growing up, moving out, or tiring of my company.

I wonder if the dog dumper knew all along it would be this way.

Kate Fratti

Little Shepherd, Guardian of Her Flock

Dogs have given us their absolute all. We are the center of their universe. We are the focus of their love and faith and trust. They serve us in return for scraps. It is without a doubt the best deal man has ever made.

Roger Caras

When I have to leave home for an hour or two, I always do so knowing my flock will be safe. It wasn't always the case. Sometimes, when I would come home from an errand in town, I would find one missing, victim to a hawk, no doubt. But since I acquired a little shepherd, I have nothing to fear. She guards her flock well!

Sidney is a shepherd mix dog. Or at least the vet thinks so. She resembles a German shepherd in shape, ears, and fur, but is much smaller, and her coloring is the prettiest blond color I have ever seen. A blondie from her head to her feet! How anyone had the heart to dump her is hard to understand, but dump her they did, right in the shopping center parking lot in town, four years ago.

I saw her when I got out of my vehicle, a sweet, friendly, half-grown puppy, running from car to car, bushy tail wagging, trying to see if anyone would want her. But I already had two dogs, and didn't need another one. I petted her head and walked away, going into the grocery store. When I came out, she was still there, greeting everyone with a "please take me home" look. But I was still determined to walk away and forget about her. Until I saw the police car pull into the parking lot, and an officer get out and approach the pup.

"Are you going to take her away?" I asked him with concern.

"Yes, ma'am. Someone called about a dog being dumped. That's why I'm here. We can't have dogs running around in the parking lot," he replied politely.

"I didn't think there was a pound here," I said.

"There isn't. This town is too small to afford a pound."

"So what will happen to the puppy?"

"Well, since we're not set up for taking care of stray dogs, it'll go to the vet and get euthanized." He picked up the pup, who was now shaking like a leaf, as if she sensed the fate in store for her.

"Well, I have just decided to adopt this pup," I said, "please put her in my truck." I opened the door.

"Are you sure, ma'am? People jump into these things, and then end up dumping these dogs again. So be sure you want to do this."

"I am quite sure. Here, I'll take her." I put the pup on the front seat of my truck.

She settled down next to me and leaned over and planted a big kiss on my face. She knew she was going to her new home.

Well, it was the best decision I've ever made. She was well received by my other two dogs, and even the cats, since they sensed she didn't have an aggressive bone in her body, and I soon named her Sidney. Sidney loved everyone around her: the other dogs, the cats, and best of all, she loved the chickens!

She ran around checking them out the first time she saw them, wagging her tail, making friendly, squealing noises at them, telling them she liked them! At first, the chickens weren't quite sure what to make of this new, enthusiastic furry arrival, but it didn't take long for them to realize she meant no harm, and was in fact their guardian and protector.

The chicken hawks around here often come to check out the menu in my yard. They do this by landing on the branch of the huge dead oak in the meadow, from where the view of the chicken doings can easily be observed. When the chickens see the hawk, they start their screech alarms, and run for cover, while I usually come sprinting out the house, broom in hand. I yell and wave my broom, until the hawk rises up and flies to another tree, hoping I'd get tired of my threats and leave, so he can come back and get lunch. I usually stay out there, waving my broom, until the hawk gives up and flies away.

Well, the first time Sidney observed me doing this, her ears perked up, and she got a glint in her eyes. Here was a job she could do. So she went racing towards the tree where the hawk was perching, barking furiously. The hawk soon decided this was too much trouble for him, and flew off to find a meal somewhere else.

"Good girl!" I praised Sidney, while the chickens calmed down and came out of hiding.

As time went on, I realized Sidney had made herself the self-appointed guardian of the flock. Every time the chickens squawked, she went running to see why. Every time a large bird landed on a nearby tree, whether it was a crow or a vulture, or even a large woodpecker, Sidney was there to make sure it didn't have evil intentions. The chickens walked around with more confidence, and I could go to town on an errand, knowing the silkies (chickens) were going to be safe in my absence. Sidney, the little shepherd takes her job as guardian very seriously!

Renie Burghardt

Shanna: A Story of Love, Devotion, and Courage

Dogs are not our whole life, but they make our lives whole.

Roger Caras

Every one of my pets is special to me. Each has brought pleasure and enlightenment into my life. I have learned something from each one and have received an abundance of love. I can only hope, on some level, I have given them a piece of what they have given to me. All have left me with a gift, a lesson, a memory. I am blessed to have had each one in my life, as I know they were a gift from God. Shanna was my first gift, and the last months of her life filled me with tremendous anguish, and personal and spiritual growth. I never expected to learn life's most intensive lessons from a dog, but I did.

Shanna was a West Highland white terrier. She was full of spunk and tenacity from the moment I saw her. As I looked at her through the window at the pet shop, she stared right into my eyes. At the moment I felt an uncanny connection. She did not break eye contact and her tail wagged furiously. She followed me as I strolled past the other dogs, almost stretching her neck to keep me in view. My heart sank, as I was unsure if I had the ability to care and be responsible for another pet. (I had two cats and two of my sister's dogs lived with us.) I left the pet store, but that dog did not leave my mind.

I returned to the store a few hours later to view my new friend once again. As I approached the window, her tail began wagging and again she was looking at me, with eyes wide, and body wiggling from the wagging of her tail. I decided it was fate. As we sat in the small "dog room" where I would sign the papers of purchase, this little white ball of fuzz raced incessantly around the chairs, grunting as she maneuvered the sharpest of turns. She would stop momentarily to jump up at me, and then continue her race. I remember thinking, "Uh-oh. I think I may be getting into more than I can handle." But it was too late, she was mine, and we left the store together.

And that's how it remained—together, forever. She went everywhere with me. We went to dog shows and training classes. She loved to perform her repertoire of tricks, and loved applause (she would proudly prance like a horse at its inception). She was a therapy dog, and helped to start a local visiting schedule to various nursing homes. Shanna loved people, other animals, and me. We were inseparable, and she was my very best friend.

Shanna was always happy. Although an occasional scolding would bring her down momentarily, she would recover quickly with a toy or a "lick" attack. I could never stay upset with her for very long, she wouldn't allow it. She knew when I didn't feel well, and would stay by my side, even refusing food. If I had a bad day, she would try anything to gain and sustain my attention, and it always worked!

As Shanna approached her thirteenth year of life, she began to have frequent bladder infections. After two courses of antibiotics, we decided to explore further possible causes. I never expected to hear and learn the outcome of her tests. Transitional cell carcinoma of the bladder was the formal diagnosis, and it was not a good prognosis. With treatment, most do not survive the year depending on the stage at diagnosis. I was heartbroken and devastated. How could my precious happy little friend be starting down the road to a grave illness? She didn't look or act ill. She showed no signs of pain or discomfort, initially. But the diagnosis was a fact; she would probably die.

Shanna had surgery on her bladder to remove the tumor with hopes of staving off the inevitable for some time. She did well with the surgery, as Shanna was Shanna. Adversity did not have an impact on her; she continued living as though the fifteen sutures in her belly were nonexistent. Shanna remained happy even as she was led down the hospital hallway for yet another blood test or x-ray. The technicians and veterinarians loved her as she would frequently wag her tail and croon her hello upon seeing them. She would lick their hands as if to console them, as they were placing the needle in her vein.

When she had to be hospitalized, I went to visit her every day. (The clinic was 35 miles away.) I had to see her, and I knew she had to see me. On one visit, the technician and I wanted to try an experiment. We decided the technician would go into the hospital ward and observe Shanna to see how long it took her to recognize I was coming to see her. The technician was amazed and noted at the very second I entered the long hallway to the ward, Shanna's head immediately perked, and she began sniffing the air. As I came closer, she began jumping and crooning. This was behind a closed door. She caught my scent and felt my presence long before I appeared. Everyone was amazed with the connections this dog made.

We began cisplantin chemotherapy which was very rough on her body. I placed a red bandana around her neck, like some chemotherapy patients wear. Shanna thought this was cool, and proudly entered the vet's office with a bellowing croon to announce her arrival. Of course, they all made a fuss. I fought back my tears as I left her there. We did not know what the outcome would be, but we had to try.

Throughout the course of Shanna's illness and treatments, I always tried to maintain a positive demeanor when I was with her. I did not speak of her illness around her, but would tell her of pending treatments or trips we would have to make. Some may think this was silly, but this dog understood so much language it was amazing. I felt if she thought I was giving up, she would too. So, I requested no one speak of the seriousness of her illness around her. I didn't want her to have any negative feelings for the road ahead, as she would need (as would I) all the courage and strength to contend with the future.

Midway through chemotherapy, she became very depressed and lethargic. This was the first time I ever saw her lose her spunk. A trip to the vet was warranted. The diagnosis was pancreatitis. She was very ill.

Within a few days of treatment she was back to her "old self" once again. She was running and playing with her other best friend, Brenna, a Scottish terrier. It seemed as if nothing had ever happened. She was happy, and it filled my heart to watch her live once again. Chemotherapy had to be stopped as obviously her system could not tolerate it. There were no other treatments. The inevitable waiting and watching would begin.

During the late spring of her thirteenth year, I found a lump on her belly. Alarmed, I immediately called the vet and took her for a visit. More bad news. She had developed a mammary tumor, and it would have to be removed as they are frequently malignant. I was warned mammary cancer was typically metastatic. Shanna had the surgery and, of course, it was malignant. I lamented inside questioning why this precious friend was being struck with yet another dismal malady. But I had to go on, for Shanna.

Brenna, my mother, and I brought Shanna home after her mammary surgery. This little white dog of fourteen pounds was sutured from her chest to the end of her belly. I believe there were forty-eight stitches. Shanna did not flinch or miss a beat. She was happy and playful, and was back to life. She amazed me with her spirit, and I envied her zeal. I remember wishing I could be like her, and face what is given with courage and strength, and a zest for life itself.

A friend had stopped by soon after her surgery, and was amazed when I showed her Shanna's belly full of sutures. She could not believe this dog was still so welcoming and happy. My friend thought we didn't have the surgery, because Shanna was so upbeat and happy. Again, at someone else's observance, I too was amazed at this little dog.

A few weeks later I discovered a little lump, on the edge of one of her bladder surgery scars. The report was not good. She had developed subcutaneous cancer on the incision. Based on all of her maladies, surgery or treatment were not options at this point. It was felt she would not do well with any type of possible treatments—one more devastating blow in the life of this wonderful creature. I was becoming numb from the inevitable. I felt there was no hope except to fill her life with love, and soak up all she had to share. And I did!

By the end of May, Shanna was healing from her mammary cancer surgery and I decided to take a "special" vacation day, just to spend it with "my girls," Shanna and Brenna. We spent the day basking in the sun, planting flowers, and wading in the small pool. This day was almost spiritual for me. I felt more of a connection with my two friends than ever before. Both of them would look at me in a way as if they were trying to relay a message, of hope, of love, of connection. I could not discern if my thoughts were self-imposed, or if perhaps the "connections" were a reality. It really didn't matter as I reveled in those feelings; I felt hope and love abounding.

A few days after our glorious special day, Shanna began to change. Sometimes she would sit and stare off into space, but would respond quickly to my voice with a wag of her tail, and a "smooch." There were times when she seemed to be in pain, as she would tremble ever so slightly, but would calm somewhat when I held her. Eating became inconsistent. I felt time with my friend was slipping away, and there was nothing I could to do save her—but she saved me in more ways than I ever thought possible! She spared me by not showing her illness overtly. She remained happy, loving, and attentive right up to the very end. She taught me to live, believe, embrace inner strength, and be happy in the moment.

As Shanna loved people and attention, I decided to have an "almost fourteen" birthday party for her. I decorated the deck with her newspaper clippings, as she was frequently photographed at local dog events. I got a cake and balloons, and invited a few friends and relatives with their dogs. Shanna, realizing something was happening out on the deck could hardly contain her excitement as she barked and paced in front of me. But I would not let her out until everyone arrived, as I wanted it to be a real surprise!

When everyone finally arrived, I opened the door for my girl, and as everyone yelled "Surprise!" she spun around barking and crooning, vivaciously wagging her tail. She went to each person, on her own, and greeted them personally. I swore this dog was human; she had such a wonderful *persona*. She enjoyed her company and the party, and was tremendously happy throughout. When the party concluded, Shanna lay on the picnic table with her party hat askew, exhausted. But she enjoyed the day, and I was happy she had so much fun.

Within a few days, Shanna began to deteriorate. Her appetite began to wane, she seemed to have difficulty breathing, and she sat more frequently.

She continued to follow me everywhere and I almost felt guilty when I moved, as I knew she was uncomfortable. She still wagged her tail, and crooned when I spoke to her, but I could see she was becoming more distressed, and weak.

Shanna did not like thunderstorms, and that summer we had them in abundance. I had purchased an air conditioner to ease the stress of the summer heat and humidity on both the dogs, and my mother and me. During one particularly violent storm we lost electricity. Shanna began to have more difficulty breathing. I placed her in my car, and we rode around town for 2½ hours until the electricity came back on. I actually relished this time with her, as I knew precious time was disappearing. She always loved to ride in the car, but she was unable to rest during this ride. I stopped at a fast food restaurant to buy her a hamburger in hopes she would eat, but she only managed one bite. We finally returned home to electricity.

Neither of us slept that night, as Shanna seemed to not want to lie down. She would just sit on the bed and stare at me. She would snuggle at my request momentarily, but then discomfort would overcome her, and she would go back to sitting and watching me. I was overridden with guilt and anguish in my thoughts of what to do for her.

Realistically I knew the time had come, but from my heart I couldn't let go. I tormented and chastised myself for being so selfish. I was exhausted, heartbroken, and distressed as I placed the call to the veterinarian's office. It was twelve midnight. Brenna, Shanna, my mother, and I loaded ourselves in the car for the emotionally heart-wrenching, thirty-five-mile-drive to the vet's office. Shanna stood in the middle of the front seats, maneuvering every turn with assured balance, as always. She even sang with me to an "oldie" on the radio. We frequently sang duets when "we" were driving. I had to stop in the middle of the song, as I choked with emotion. I still didn't want to cry in front of her. I wept silently. She looked at me in question, touching her nose to mine, as she did so often. My consolation, she knew.

The doctor was waiting for us as we arrived. Shanna leaped out of the car crooning hello to the doctor and wagging her tail. I secretly prayed this was not the end, and the doctor would be able to provide some comfort. As the doctor examined Shanna, her eyes filled with tears. I covered Shanna's ears, as I had done so often so she wouldn't hear negative statements.

The doctor explained there was barely any air going through her lungs, it was time, the Lasix was no longer working. The most emotional moment in my life came barreling in at that second. The doctor and I tried to fight back tears as Shanna wagged her tail in my arms. The doctor asked me if I was ready. I nodded, and held onto my girl, telling her I loved her. Within moments she slumped in my arms, and I cried like a baby. I told her I was sorry, as I sobbed hysterically. I held her and loved her for the final time.

I cried for six months, especially when it was time for bed, as she and Brenna always slept in the bed with me. I missed her next to me. Brenna missed her too; from that point on she never slept on the bed again. She would not stay; she slept on the floor at the bottom of the bed. Brenna was in mourning too, as she and Shanna were inseparable. The neighbors would tell me how Brenna cried during the day. She was lonely and missed her friend. Brenna and I frequently visited Shanna's grave at the cemetery, and Brenna would just sit and stare. I wondered what she really thought, but I knew she missed her friend.

Life for Brenna and me was one of loss and grieving. Shanna was not around the corner, she was gone. I can truthfully say I was probably clinically depressed at losing my friend. But during this time I also had several revelations within myself. I had a renewal of spirit and hope as I contemplated what this little white dog gave me, through her spirit, courage, and devotion. She was an extraordinary teacher, and she showed me how to love and live unconditionally. Shanna taught me to look for the positive, because being positive eases the burdens of today, and tomorrow. A bright spot is always radiated, when I think of her. It is visual, I can see it, but most of all I can feel it. Shanna had a power, a strength, and fortitude. She was a gift and blessing from God. I am forever grateful for her, and one day hope to see her again.

During the months following Shanna's death, Brenna began to fall ill. Once again we began our search for a cause and, hopefully, treatment. She was hospitalized off and on for several weeks, having biopsies, x-rays, and other diagnostics, but nothing definitive was presented or discovered.

Finally at a point of no return, the doctor requested to perform an exploratory surgery. Reluctantly I consented. As I waited in the waiting room during her surgery, I was summoned to the operating room. The doctor told me she was full of cancer, the needle biopsies had missed the exact spots. There was no hope for recovery.

As I held her in my arms while she remained under anesthesia, the doctor injected her. She died in my arms. Shanna and Brenna were together again. This time, it is forever!

I lost my friends within six months of each other. My house, and my heart, were empty. The gifts I received live on within me today. I cherish their memory and hold them close in my heart. I never thought I would learn from my pets. But I did.

I tell my friends, "People can learn a lot from a dog," and I smile as I think of "my girls."

Dana Smith-Mansell

What's That Noise?

My idea of good poetry is any dog doing anything.
J. Allen Boone

My Simon is a "fraidy" dog. He doesn't like loud noises, strangers, or being awakened. He's becoming one of those dogs that mumbles under his breath as he gets older; the grumpy old man in the canine domain. One thing he will stay awake for is a ride in the truck. True to dachshund form, he loves to be up high. He sits on the console and keeps watch for danger as we go down the road. Being a beautiful black dappled miniature dachshund, he draws attention wherever we take him. But I warn people away. He is skittish I tell them while trying to hold him back as he growls and lunges at all admirers.

What I don't say is this ferocious attack dog is afraid of his own bodily noises. I wonder some days if he doesn't think the house is haunted and he is the focus of all the ghostly efforts. He will lay beneath a blanket with only his nose and eyes visible, watching for anything that may be out to get him.

He's reached that age when his dog-job is to sleep all the time. And let me tell you, he is extremely good at his job, a real professional. However, because of his attention to the details of his job, I don't think he gets enough exercise. So his food moves slowly in his digestive tract and creates gas. Then he passes it. And when he does, it isn't just a little wind, a poof, if you will. No, his bodily function can be heard in the next room. And these noises startle him. He jumps up and looks to see what snuck up behind him. Then, seeing nothing, or no one, he slinks off to burrow beneath the nearest blanket or throw. If he happens to be standing, he takes off like he's being chased by Satan and seeks the comfort of a confined hiding spot, like behind the clothes in the bedroom closet. It usually takes a human effort to coax him out.

The odor, although it wakes Simon up, doesn't seem to bother him as much. He does leave the area, because, after all, who wants to sit in stinky air? But when he gets up, he shakes his tail and more or less saunters away. Often, he shoots us a look of annoyance. He wants to be sure we know someone did something in his space to disturb him and it doesn't make him happy. Obviously he doesn't recognize the part he played in the situation.

Although it is funny to watch sometimes, I worry my dog is going to be driven mad by his own gas. I wonder if I could find a way to just get him to understand this bodily function. A way I could get him to accept the noises as a normal part of his life. I can envision him passing gas, stretching out long and hard, and smirking like most of the males I know. I don't appreciate that behavior in the human males in the household, but I would welcome it from Simon. He would be free from the gas demons and I wouldn't have to worry about his mental health.

Elaine Whitesides

Forever Faithful: Shep's Story

There is no faith which has never yet been broken, except that of a truly faithful dog.

Konrad Lorenz

In April 2001, I found myself wandering through remote northern Montana. I was writing an article on Lewis and Clark, and following their epic trail of discovery across country that remains nearly as remote and unspoiled today as it was in their time.

Though the calendar said spring had arrived, Montana was still pretty wintry. One cold snowy afternoon, I arrived at the northern end of my journey, Fort Benton on the Upper Missouri River. I spent several days in that delightful, friendly little town.

In Fort Benton I came across what has to be one of the greatest stories ever told of canine love and loyalty. The next few days the story of Shep unfolded and came alive for me, though he'd been dead nearly sixty years.

Shep became a legend in his own lifetime. And now that he's gone, his legend continues growing and touching the hearts of all who hear his story.

During the summer of 1936, a sheepherder fell ill while tending his flock and was brought to St. Clare Hospital in Fort Benton, Montana. A nondescript sheep dog had followed the herder into town and soon set up a vigil at the hospital's door. A kindhearted nun who ran the hospital kitchen fed the dog during those few days before the man died. The herder's family in the East requested his body be sent back home.

On that August day the undertaker put the body on the eastbound train for shipment to his waiting relatives. As the gurney was rolled out onto the platform, a big gaunt shepherd dog with watchful eyes appeared out of nowhere and watched as the casket was loaded into the baggage car. Attendants later recalled the dog whining as the door slammed shut and the engine slowly started pulling away from the station, then head down, turning and trotting down the tracks. On that day the dog, later named Shep, began a 5½-year vigil broken only by his own death.

Day after day, meeting four trains daily, Shep became a fixture on the platform. He eyed each passenger hopefully, and was often chased off as a mongrel, but never completely discouraged. Neither the heat of summer days nor the bitter Montana winter days prevented Shep from meeting the next train. As Shep's fame spread, people came from everywhere to see him, to photograph him, and to try and make friends and possibly adopt him. All of the attention was somewhat unwelcome; after checking the train he often retired quickly to get away from those who came to see him.

Most people missed the point Shep was a one-man dog. The bond he had formed with the herder many years before was simply the most important thing in his life. Food, shelter, and attention were now provided by the railroad employees. That was all he wanted, except his master's return.

Shep was an older dog when he came to the station house in Fort Benton. Throughout his vigil the long nights under the platform and the cold winter had taken their toll. Stiff-legged and hard of hearing, Shep failed to hear old 235 as it rolled into the station at 10:17 that cold winter morning of January 12, 1942. He turned to look when the engine was almost upon him, moved to get out of the way, and slipped on the icy rails. Shep's long vigil had ended.

Shep's funeral was held two days later. He was laid to rest on the high windy bluff overlooking the station where his long wait had been in vain. The sights and sounds of the singing rails and the whistles around the bend are all gone now, also passing with time.

No passenger trains pull into the station today, but Shep still maintains his lonely vigil atop the wind-swept bluff overlooking the abandoned depot.

Shep's Eulogy

George Graham Vest was a 19th century lawyer and United States Senator from Missouri. In 1870 he took on a client whose dog had been killed by a neighbor. During the trial, Vest vowed he would "win the case or apologize to every dog in Missouri." His closing argument which won the case, has come to be known as "Eulogy to a Dog."

Reverend Ralph Underwood, minister of Fort Benton's First Christian Church, presided at Shep's funeral service and gave the eulogy, excerpted from Senator Vest's closing argument. It's a fitting final tribute to Shep and to all our loyal and loving canine friends.

> The one absolutely unselfish friend that a man can have in this selfish world, the one that never deserts him and the one that never proves ungrateful or treacherous is his dog.
>
> A man's dog stands by him in prosperity and in poverty, in health and in sickness. He will sleep on the cold ground, where the wintry winds blow and the snow drives fiercely, if only he may be near his master's side. He will kiss the hand that has no food to offer, he will lick the wounds and sores that come in encounters with the roughness of the world. He guards the sleep of his pauper master as if he were a prince. When all other friends desert, he remains.
>
> When riches take wings and reputation falls to pieces, he is as constant in his love as the sun in its journey through the heavens. If fortune drives the master forth an outcast in the world, friendless and homeless, the faithful dog asks no higher privilege than that of accompanying him to guard against danger, to fight against his enemies, and when the last scene of all comes, and death takes the master in its embrace and his body is laid away in the cold ground, no matter if all other friends pursue their

way, there by his graveside will the noble dog be found, his head between his paws, his eyes sad but open in alert watchfulness, faithful and true even to death.

The River and Plains Society with introduction by John Cali

Princess: The Mutt with Moxie

Apply dog logic to life: eat well, be loved, get petted, sleep a lot and dream of a leash-free world.

Susan Ariel Rainbow Kennedy

I first laid eyes on Princess, the great Dane-boxer-German shepherd and/or mutt, one evening in March 1971. She was three years old, and if not for my last-minute reprieve, would have been on her way to the county humane society. Apparently her previous owner had bred her, kept her pups, and then decided to dump her. If a soft-hearted friend of mine had not taken her in until she could palm her off on me, this unique and loveable mutt might never have become part of my family.

Our relationship began the night my old school chum, Lynn, called me and explained Princess' plight. I responded quickly and without hesitation—"Sure, bring her over." After I hung up, however, I began having second thoughts. What if this dog is sickly—or mean or weird? (I found I was right on the third count.)

When the doorbell rang, I jumped. Taking a deep breath, I walked over to the door and opened it. I looked down on what appeared to be a small horse. One pointy ear stood up on its head, while the other hung forlornly down. An odd blend of stripes ran up and down its lanky body. "Oh," I said. I could've kicked myself for not asking more questions earlier about this goofy-looking mutt.

"So come in," I said slowly, not sure I could successfully slam the door without doing serious damage to the two hairy front paws already planted in my doorway.

Panting and slobbering, Princess entered my domain for the first time.

It didn't take long for Princess' true personality to emerge. Looking at her strictly from a physical point of view, she appeared to be, simply, a dog. One might even assume she was a vicious dog. Nothing could have been farther from the truth. She was a full-fledged coward. Show her a broom, and she would take off at break-neck speed, hiding behind the first piece of furniture she could find.

Why? I never knew. Nevertheless, the broom quickly became my weapon of choice.

Thunderstorms were another source of pure terror for Princess. At the first crack of thunder, she would high-tail it to her "safe place," which happened to be underneath my bed. No amount of tugging or pulling on her rigid legs could get her to budge once she had "dug" in. Stubbornness, I found, was another of this mutt's not-so-endearing traits.

I also discovered one of Princess' favorite pastimes—when no one was around—was to paw through the garbage. She was amazingly careful about how she went about this delicate operation. Very gently, piece by piece, she would systematically remove the contents of the trash container, laying all the items on the floor. Then she would continue to dig further until she came across something edible. This could be anything with a remote scent of food on it; a gum wrapper would do.

One day, I secretly observed her as she indulged in this favorite ritual. I had to admire her diligence. She was good. She was very good.

Seeing how engrossed she was in the task before her, I slowly crept up on her, holding my breath, and hoping I could catch her off-guard. I did. Shouting, "What are you doing?" I scared the living daylights out of her. She whipped her head up from inside the trash container and looked at me with shock and disbelief, not to mention terror. Old soggy coffee grounds clung to her whiskers, a splatter of ketchup sat on the tip of her black nose. She knew she was in trouble. So she did what she always did when in these circumstances: she threw herself on the floor, stretched out her front and hind legs, and did her famous belly crawl. Hence, came her nickname—Sneaky Snake.

Sneaky Snake lived up to her name on one particular Christmas. I will never forget that day. I had put special effort into baking cookies that year, so I fussed over arranging them just right on the platters so they looked pretty and festive for the company we were expecting. I also put out an impressive assortment of candies and cheeses—all ready for our guests' consumption. My only mistake was leaving Princess in the presence of such temptation, while we went downstairs to the recreation room.

We were gone too long.

As I walked upstairs sometime later, I had the eerie sense of something being awry. It was way too quiet. Princess, usually at my heels, was nowhere in sight. (Always a bad sign.) I could feel butterflies flitting merrily in my stomach as I approached the living room. Then, I saw the unimaginable: The cocktail table, once laden with mouth-watering goodies, was now bare—only a few empty plates remained. All the cookies were gone. All the candies and cheeses were gone. Even the dip had been "dipped" into.

The glutton had devoured the whole works.

I screamed.

One by one, family members came running into the living room, huffing and puffing from racing up the stairs. They gathered around—all staring in disbelief at the empty living room, at the empty table.

"Oh my," said my mother.

"Oh, dear," said my mother-in-law.

"Oh, oh," said my youngest daughter.

"I'll get the broom," said my oldest daughter from the back of the room. I could only nod in the affirmative.

In another room not far away, a dog with a belly full of stolen treats lay cowering.

Christmas wasn't the only holiday Princess partook in. She enjoyed a certain Easter as well. It was the Easter our son, Brian, turned two. Brian had decided to do a little "bonding" with his furry friend that Easter Sunday, behind the big chair in the living room, alone—secretly.

I had been busy in the dining room, setting the table for our usual Easter dinner, when I thought I heard a strange noise. It was a soft crackling sound. Puzzled, I stopped what I was doing and looked around. I couldn't see anything out of the ordinary, so I continued with my business.

Crack. There it was again. I paused once more, straining my ears to hear.

Crack crack. What in the world is that? I wondered.

CRACK!

Now I could tell where it was coming from. Quietly, I tip-toed over to the big chair across the room, and peeked over the top. There they sat, son and dog. A bowl of colored hard-boiled eggs sat between them—a pile of egg shells sat next to them. My son and his partner in crime looked solemnly up at me.

"Oh, no," I whispered. It was obvious my son had been cracking and peeling the eggs, feeding them one by one to the eager recipient Princess.

Needless to say, for the next few days, maybe longer, I kept several windows open throughout the house. Princess slunk around wearing a perpetual look of guilt as she expelled gaseous vapors from her overindulgence in boiled Easter eggs.

"You stink," became a popular refrain around our house.

There were other holidays throughout the years, each, in their own way, special. It's funny, how a mere mutt could make the difference between ordinary times and extraordinary times; how one, goofy, exasperating, and unpredictable dog could bring such utter joy and laughter to otherwise mundane experiences. Princess could. That was her job. She made the days a little brighter and the nights a little shorter.

Perhaps just a dog to some, but to me she was a fur-wrapped gift of pure love. I can see her still, wearing her famous "stupid" look; that expression she wore just before she was "found out." I can see her happy look, her sad look, her frightened look. But I had never seen a mean look. She didn't possess one.

Princess lived with our family for ten wonderful years before passing from cancer. We miss her still.

Nancy Ilk

Max, My Beloved Schnauzer

Dogs are miracles with paws.

Susan Ariel Rainbow Kennedy

Maximillan McElligott was a pure bred, AKC-registered, miniature schnauzer. Of the many dogs we had as pets, Max had been the most special little guy in my life. Even though he has been dead for several years, I'll never forget him.

Max came to live with my wife and me when our daughter, for whom he had been purchased as a puppy, went off to basic training in the US Air Force. Max quickly became my best friend. I am an epileptic and I'll always remember the times he was at my side when my medicines were not controlling my seizures, which resulted in me suffering numerous falls and injuries.

I quickly learned Max had a dual character, depending upon his situation. If he was in our home, I could practically guarantee he'd be at my side, my greatest friend. On the other hand, when outside, the only assurance I had was Max would immediately forsake me in favor of his other "best friends" of nature.

Whether his extraordinary senses perceived another dog, (size was irrelevant), a beckoning tree, or a fire hydrant, I would be left in his dust. By the time we were both exhausted from the "fun" of the chase, I was swearing I'd never again drop his leash, along with other choice words I can't repeat here.

Back in the house, Max would spend his first few moments glued to the side of my wife, Joan. After all, she kept his food and water bowls filled to the brim.

Much of the rest of his day Max would be planted next to my desk as I worked. He seemed to "know" before anyone else when one of my seizures was coming on. He could not prevent them, but on several occasions after I regained consciousness (always unhurt, thank God), I found Max licking my face. Often, he would play

German shepherd and refuse to allow paramedics near me until Joan convinced Max they, like him, were there to help Dad.

I recall the occasion when I had fallen on ice in the driveway and spent several days in the hospital having my left hip fracture repaired. Max seemed lost—rather, he thought he had lost his dearest companion. He spent every day looking out the front window of our living room, waiting for me to come home.

Finally, I was released from the hospital and sent home after we had hospital equipment set up for my return and continued therapy. Joan reminded me of the craziness with Max when paramedics tried to bring my stretcher in the narrow front door of the house we were renting. It was bad enough they had to turn the stretcher, but in his excitement, Max was jumping up to reach his long-gone master, nearly causing the ambulance driver to drop me onto the hardwood floor.

When Joan realized Max was on the verge of sending me back to the hospital, she scooped him into her arms and I finally arrived home safely. Max spent the next hour snuggling up to me, telling me how much he missed my presence. Next to the hugs and kisses from my parents, my wife and my children, I had never before felt such love.

Although Max has been gone almost nine years (it seems more like fifteen), I still think about him when I see another dog with his or her owner. Even after those times I might have been overly harsh in correcting him for his outside behavior, Max would always be at my side when I needed him.

Joan and I were blessed when our veterinarian gave Max added years of life by simply pulling his bad teeth. To all owners of miniature schnauzers, I highly recommend you maintain your pet's dental health, the importance of which I did not understand during Max's lifetime.

The day finally came when our vet told us Max could hardly see any more and was in almost constant pain with cancerous tumors. No matter how kind it was supposed to sound, I found it terribly hard to be told we would be more loving toward our adored pet if we were to free him from his pain and blindness.

Our vet advised us we would be more kind to Max by allowing him to euthanize Max, put him to sleep. Due to my own illnesses, I've had many falls and injuries, but I never had such a broken heart as on the day Joan took Max to the vet for the last time. Even as I write this, I have tears falling on my cheeks.

For those seeking a kind and loving pet, I can honestly say a miniature schnauzer is the dog you want for yourself and your family.

Walter McElligott

Walter McElligott

The Happiest Dog at Christmas

To err is human, to forgive, canine.

Unknown

I don't know what drives so many dog owners to tease their pets. By teasing, I mean antics—not the kind of sickening animal cruelty you see on the six o'clock news. Rather, harmless bits, such as dressing your beagle up like Santa Claus, or getting your poodle to bear her teeth upon an odd signal you thought up, or that false knock at the door that works your pooch into a frenzy.

Luckily, our dogs take our waggish behavior in stride for no other reason than to patiently wait for that pat on the head, that endearing esteem-building praise and, of course, the loftiest reward of all—a treat to eat. Then, they endure one last time our howls of laughter over our canine's special performance. Our dogs put up with a lot of shenanigans from us, but it's good clean fun as long as he's wagging his tail, right?

I hope I'm not the worst offender on the planet for the doggie practical joke, though I know I came fairly close one time.

A Christmas never passes in our house that my wife and I don't put a gift (or two, or three) under the tree for our pets. Our miniature schnauzer, Otto, who left us years ago, actually opened his own gifts. He would tear the paper away with no less diligence than a four-year old child might. And we have the pictures to prove it. All our miniature schnauzers throughout the years have shared the Christmas tradition of opening gifts with us. Perhaps it's embedded in the racial memory of their genes. After all, much of the Christmas tradition comes from the schnauzer's homeland. I've often wondered if a fantastic theory lurks somewhere out there that's not yet formulated.

With that thought in mind, I'll now tell you about a Christmas with our last miniature schnauzer, Hannah. I decided to pull a little prank on her, and of course, to experiment with the hypothesis she

77

really did feel something at Christmas and there was (or was not) something to this doggie-gift-giving business.

The pile of gifts finally dwindled to but a few under the tree. Hannah watched tentatively from the comfort of her easy chair. My wife and I exchanged another gift and by then the tree looked nearly barren. Hannah turned away feigning disinterest. I knew she was bluffing. Otherwise she would have left the room. From my perspective, the experiment was proceeding nicely. She was waiting for her gift.

The moment was ripe for the tease.

"I guess that's all there is," I said to my wife.

I turned to Hannah and said, "Sorry, old girl, looks like we forgot to get you anything this year." I shrugged my shoulders, palms up.

A knave can never get enough. So for good measure, I added, "Maybe, just maybe, you've been a bad girl this year."

She snorted and turned away. I hope scientists one day will explain how it is we are able to read our dog's emotions in his or her face. Hannah's read pure disgust.

Then came the point where I deserved a good butt-kicking. I spied another gift under the tree. With all the drama of an old geezer who acts his first bit part in a community theater production (after unsuccessfully auditioning for years on end), I exclaimed, "Wait a minute. I see one more present. Let's see who this is for."

Hannah's nubby little tail wagged frenetically. She stood up in her seat and stretched toward the tree. If she could have talked she surely would have said, "Oh thank you, Daddy!"

(Here's where the boot meets the butt.)

"Oh—it's for Mommy."

I doubt a veterinarian would ever admit dogs shed tears from sadness. They'll admit dogs grieve, moan from a broken heart, and surely mope—but not cry. However, I will tell them and the whole world they are dead wrong. Hannah's eyes watered and then a tear trickled down each cheek into her beard. Her face read utter heartbreak. My throat got all lumpy. I thought Santa might crash down the chimney, pack up all my presents, and cart them away.

I could abide in no more "experiments" or canine practical jokes. I hurried over to the tree, snatched up a gift cleverly hidden under a fold of the tree skirt, and then gave it to Hannah.

"Here, sweetie, from Mommy and Daddy."

Hannah understandably displayed a moment of hesitation. Yet within the next beat, she stood on her feet nuzzling the present, her tail wagging without cessation. I assisted my little baby in getting her gift opened: one of her favorite doggie treats she received only at Christmas, kind of like chocolate covered cherries for pups.

My wife stood close by with another present. After we opened that gift for her, she stretched her front legs onto our shoulders, gratefully nestled her head under our chins, and gave us a good cheek slathering with her tongue. She jumped from the chair with a treat firmly in her mouth and headed off somewhere inside the house to enjoy it—in peace.

I think about Hannah often. I tell her successor, a miniature schnauzer named Fitzgerald, what a wonderful dog she was and how much he would have loved her. And I think about the lesson she taught me about compassion. Yet most of all, I await the day when the two of us will cross the Rainbow Bridge together and I'll learn one last lesson from Hannah—forgiveness.

Robert Paul Blumenstein

The Compassion of a Dog

A dog is not almost-human, and I know of no greater insult to the canine race than to describe it as such.

John Holmes

Shane was a Scottish terrier and took great pride in guarding his domain. He loved to sit on the porch (tied of course) and enjoyed guarding the house. One morning we heard a commotion outside where Shane was sitting. As we approached the door, we saw the neighbor's grandchildren throwing rocks and sticks at Shane. Shane was very upset and was growling and barking at them. We brought Shane inside to calm him. We spoke to the neighbors and they assured us "it would never happen again." Unfortunately, from that point on Shane decided not to trust any young children, and would go into protective mode whenever he saw them.

The neighbor with the unruly grandchildren eventually moved away and a middle-aged couple moved in. They had a grandchild who had special challenges and attended a special school. Whenever the children were around we always made sure we were with Shane or brought him inside.

Upon returning home from a shopping trip, we saw the neighbor having a picnic for the children from their grandchild's school. There were children crawling on the ground, children running, and children in wheelchairs. They were having a grand time laughing and playing.

As we walked up on the porch, we saw somehow our side door was open—Shane was nowhere to be found. We search and called, but we could not find him.

Frantic, we realized he must be outside—the children! As we fumbled down the porch steps, we heard the children calling, "Here doggie, here doggie." We called to our neighbor to get the dog—she waved us over. As we approached, hearts pounding, we saw Shane wandering from child to child, receiving pats on the head and treats from his new friends. The neighbor laughed and said, "He's been over here all day. He's been great with the children."

In shock we watched as our Shane who did not like children, mingled safely and openly with the children from the school. Who says animals don't understand?

Dana Smith-Mansell

Our Guardian

A good dog never dies, he always stays; he walks beside you on crisp autumn days when frost is on the fields and winter's drawing near, his head is within our hand in his old way.

Mary Carolyn Davies

I've always shared my space with dogs and cats. For those of us who have lived with pets in our lives, it is only natural some of them become extra special to us. Perhaps it was the family dog that shared your childhood, or a pet that hovered nearby, giving comfort during a particularly rough time. Every pet owner has favorites. My dog, Mardi, was such an animal.

The year was 1972. I was in my twenties, a "flower child" of the era, living with my boyfriend, demonstrating against the war and rebelling against many of the values my parents held dear. The love affair ended and I found myself living alone with only a cat and my little dog, Nathaniel, for company. Feeling safe in the run-down neighborhood where I lived hadn't been an issue when my boyfriend lived with me, but once he was gone, I began to be fearful and dreaded going home at night. I couldn't afford to move, so I started thinking about getting another dog—a big one.

I saw an ad in the paper for a six-month-old red and rust, female Doberman pinscher and decided to go have a look. She was bred for the show ring by people who had been showing their beautiful Dobermans for years. They had more dogs than they had room and were forced to choose between this female and her brother. One of them would be groomed to become a champion show dog, the other would be sold for a reasonable price to someone they believed would provide a good home. The family's last name was Henlon and they had named her Henlon's Mardigras in Red. Although I was an impoverished hippie woman and could ill afford a $200 dog, I knew from the moment I saw her, I had to make her mine.

Convincing the Henlon family I was a good choice as her guardian wasn't easy. My hippie clothes put them off, I'm sure. They had to be wondering if this young woman with the beads and wild Janis Joplin hair would really take good care of their big, rambunctious pup. Yet, it was obvious Mardi and I had an instant rapport. It was a strange scene as I sat for hours convincing this middle-class family to let me give them my rent money for their dog. In the end, they let me load her into my old car, and Mardi and I went home.

We became inseparable and except when I was working, spent every minute together. She instantly settled in as my protector and pal. I was working in a bar at the time and I would come home in the middle of the night and take her and my little terrier-mix out for long meandering walks, no longer fearful of anyone or anything. Nathaniel, my "tiny" doggie companion, was jealous at first, but gradually, he too, began to view her as a guardian angel in our lives. He became a snippy little bully on the darkened streets, barking at strangers and other dogs, something he'd never done until he had Mardi for muscle to back him.

I visited the Henlon family a few months later so they could see their decision to sell her to me had been a good one. When I pulled into their driveway, Mardi immediately jumped out of the car and began sniffing around the front yard. I didn't have a leash on her; didn't need one as she always stayed close and came immediately when I called. But the Henlon's dogs, because there were so many, didn't have the same kind of bond with them. And when they opened their front door and saw Mardi running loose, they became panic-stricken, thinking she might bolt at any second. I was puzzled at their concern. "She won't go anywhere," I assured them and with one snap of my fingers, she was instantly at my side. That was, I'm sure, the defining moment when I completely won them over and our friendship was sealed.

When I became pregnant with my son a couple years later, people warned me a baby wouldn't be safe with that "vicious" dog in my house. It's true, she was very protective of me and didn't much care for strangers, but she was always polite and gentle with my friends and whenever she took a dislike to someone, her instincts always proved to be on target.

The day I brought my son, Adam, home from the hospital, I sat down with her and let her sniff him, telling her he was my baby and belonged to us. I can't explain why she wasn't jealous or how she knew Adam was part of me, but she did. She would park herself outside my bedroom when he was sleeping and if anyone came to see us, even my mom, she wouldn't allow them near him until I told her it was okay.

As Adam grew, I never worried about him running into the street or being abducted when he played outside. Our big, red pal ran a tight ship and was always careful our boy was safe.

In 1985, four days before Christmas, Mardi, after having hip problems for years, became completely incapacitated. I got up that morning and found her shivering in pain and unable to walk. I had known she was failing for months, but the reality she could no longer go on was a crushing blow. I called my vet, and although it was Sunday, he met me at his office. There, as I sat sobbing with her head in my lap, he administered a shot, mercifully ending her suffering.

I cried my way through the holidays that year, but folks in my life were hard-pressed to understand the depth of my grief. My son and the rest of my family mostly understood, but friends viewed my tears with bewilderment and urged me to cheer up; it was, after all, the happy holiday season. It's easy to comprehend the sorrow and sympathize when someone mourns a human death, but for many, it is more difficult to fathom the heavy-heartedness an owner feels when their pet dies.

I had her cremated, and to this day, the tin containing her ashes sits on a bookshelf in my house. Every once in awhile, all these years later, she still occasionally turns up in one of my dreams. My sweet girl. She always appears young and beautiful in the nether world of REM with her glistening red coat and her sparkling eyes as she cocks her head or licks my hand, my forever friend.

Susanne Fogle

An Angel Named Taffy

The dog represents all that is best in man.

Etienne Charlet

Taffy is a mixed-breed mutt dressed in a long, thick reddish-blond coat. She's a small dog whose hair streams out behind her when she is racing at top speed, like golden ripples of sunlight. The love that shines from her expressive dark brown eyes melts my heart. And up until a few summers ago, she had strictly been a one-person dog. Mine.

To say she was unfriendly would be an understatement. She was never mean to anybody, but she sure was standoffish. And as for Taffy and my teen-aged daughter, Laura, forget it. Their relationship oozed sibling rivalry from Day One. Taffy wanted nothing to do with Laura, and Laura wanted nothing to do with her!

Then something happened that shattered our family. Laura's cousin died in a grinding traffic accident. She and Laura were closer than sisters, and best friends to boot. Laura was devastated.

After the funeral, my active, vivacious daughter withdrew and became silent and pale. She refused to go out with friends and wouldn't even talk on the phone. She didn't eat at all, and began spending long hours alone in her room. My heart ached for her. Her deep depression was frightening and I didn't know how to help.

One day as I sat working at the computer in the living room, I heard a scratch at the front door and went to investigate. There stood Taffy on the porch mat, staring through the screen door into the house. "What is it, girl?" I asked. For the first time in her life, she ignored me. She leaned to one side to peer around me and then raised a shaggy paw to scratch the door again. Puzzled, I opened it a crack to pet her. She glanced up at me, dodged my hand, and made as if to squeeze inside.

"No, girl," I said, and closed the door. She whined and pawed the screen again. "Crazy dog," I muttered.

Taffy maintained her vigil at the door. She whimpered and growled, paced back and forth, and from time to time pawed at the screen. Whenever I went to the door, she adamantly ignored me. Whatever she wanted, it definitely wasn't me!

Soon I heard Laura stirring around down the hall. Taffy, who had settled into an uneasy position on the doormat, sprang to her feet and began clawing the screen again. When Laura walked into the living room, Taffy yipped excitedly and danced from side to side. I glanced at Laura, who looked as confused as I felt. "What's wrong with her, Mom?" she asked.

"Beats me," I replied. "She's been acting weird all day."

I went to the door again. Impatiently, Taffy sidestepped so she could see around me. She focused her gaze on Laura and started to softly, insistently dog-speak to her through the screen.

I opened the door, expecting Taffy to do her usual thing: jump all over me and want to play. Instead, she streaked past me without so much as a friendly tail wag in my direction, and bounded straight to Laura. Laura had stretched out on the couch and Taffy sprang up beside her, did a half turn, then plopped down. She laid her head in Laura's lap and gently placed one paw on her arm. With her cold, wet nose, she nudged Laura's hand.

"Mom!" Laura exclaimed. She stroked Taffy's long silky coat. "Do you see this? She's never done this before!"

I stared in amazement as the small dog nuzzled Laura and then snuggled in beside her as if they were old friends. Taffy, who had never willingly let Laura touch her, was now insisting on full body contact. As I watched my daughter caress Taffy's head and comb her fingers through the dog's hair, an expression crept across her pale, sad face that did my heart good. For the first time in days, Laura smiled.

Laura and Taffy cuddled on the sofa all afternoon. Taffy vocalized the whole time, growling, whining, and yipping in her insistent doggy style. Though she didn't speak in words we could understand, there was no mistaking her meaning.

The same expression was in the little dog's gaze I had only seen before when she looked at me. Love shone from her eyes as she smiled up at Laura. She snuggled her shaggy little body against my daughter and encircled her bruised spirit with a blanket of love so real it was almost visible.

Do angels always appear in human form? Maybe they do for some people. But that summer, when Laura needed an angel the most, one came to her dressed in the shape of a small, standoffish mixed-breed mutt named Taffy.

Anne C. Watkins

My Amazing Dog Thunder Bear

Our perfect companions never have fewer than four feet.

Colette

My late dog Thunder Bear was an odd-looking dog, part beagle, part basset, part German shepherd, and goodness knows what else. She had very short legs and a large voice, great heart, and was incredibly intelligent and a wonderful protector.

Bear came to us as a baby, and at first I was uncertain how the cats would react as it had been over three years since Tila, the male cat, had lived with a dog, and my young female cat, Clea, had never done so.

The cats took to Bear right away, understanding how young she was, playing with her, and in many ways they taught her to be a cat instead of a dog.

I had to lock Clea in the house when I took Bear for a walk or she would follow us to keep watch over her "baby."

Clea also delighted in getting Bear to chase her to a large planter, would circle it and jump in and then peak over the top as the puppy raced around and around the planter, trying to figure out where the cat had gone.

Bear learned a lot from the cats, and one evening she wanted to sit next to me on the couch, but Tila was already there, so Bear went and got her squeak toy and stood next to where the cat was sleeping and mouthed the toy so it squeaked over and over again. The cat's ears went back, and he hunched and suddenly jumped up and left.

Bear immediately dropped her toy and got up where Tila had been.

One afternoon I was sitting at the bottom of a u-shaped couch while my son Phil and his friend Brent sat on the two legs across from each other, tossing a small ball back and forth.

Bear desperately wanted to play ball as well, but her legs were so short and her body so heavy, she could not reach the ball as it flew over her head. So, in one seemingly impossible effort, she launched herself up and managed to hit the ball with her nose, and it bounded into my lap.

We were all so delighted and laughing and praising her, and from that time on Bear would play "catch," but instead of catching the ball in her mouth, she would hit it with her nose, and with great accuracy get it back to the person who had thrown it.

Bear's most astonishing act was when she saved me from the scorpion.

One evening we were in the back yard, walking around the swimming pool, and in the moonlight I saw a small dark object on the pool decking.

Bear went over to it and then went up in the air like a chess knight, making a seemingly impossible move given her stubby legs—up, then a straight line perpendicular in the air, and then down away from the object, and I immediately had a flash of a picture of a scorpion in my mind.

I had been barefoot and ran in for my shoes and a flashlight and discovered that indeed it was a scorpion.

In sending me the mental image of the danger near my bare feet, Thunder Bear gave me a wonderful lesson in animals as our guardians and protectors.

Bear died at age nine after valley fever had settled in her spine. I was with her at the end, stroking her velvety ears. And I still miss and remember her with great respect and love.

Judith Anderson

A Sight to Behold

When there is great love, there are always miracles.

Willa Cather

It was a very emotional month, August 2002. My mother's physical condition was deteriorating. I longed for a sign she was improving, but it was not to be. After literally spending her last twenty- four hours by my mother's side in the hospital, I came home—shattered, torn, and lost. My mother had passed away. I was greeted by my three dogs, but barely had the strength or emotion to enjoy their welcome. As odd as it may sound, I told them Mom was not coming home any more. When I said that they looked at me sort of quizzically, but I didn't really think much about their response, or my interpretation. After completing our nightly dog ritual of potty time and a treat, we all climbed into bed. My heart was heavy, and it seemed they all knew it as they stayed exceptionally close.

I didn't sleep well that night and therefore my husband, I, and the dogs were up very early. I knew I had phone calls to make. I was so distraught with the loss of my mother I felt as if I was walking through a vacuum. She and I, and the dogs, had lived together for most of my life, and when I married, my husband joined our home. Without her I felt a huge void and emptiness.

We had just purchased a new chair for her, as her old recliner had seen better days. As my husband and I stood conversing in the living room, the same room where her chair was, Trevar our young Scottie began furiously wagging his tail and flattening his ears against his head. Without obvious provocation (to us), he was very excited. Since he was making such a fuss, we stopped to watch him. He eagerly jumped up on my mother's chair, wagging his tail and holding his ears flat against his head. He was so happy and was all but turning inside out with zeal.

My husband and I struggled to figure out what he was doing and why. We looked behind the chair, on the wall, and I even went so far as to go outdoors to see if something was outside the door. We saw nothing.

Trevar's joy continued as he stepped to the arm of the chair, still wagging his tail. He stopped on the edge still furiously wagging his tail, intent on watching something—he was elated and filled with excitement. His head movements showed us he was intent, as he did not break his vision, nor was he aware of our presence. My husband and I were perplexed by his behavior, but nonetheless intrigued as we watched him.

He definitely saw something, but what? He followed his vision, stretching his neck upward. Suddenly he jumped off the chair, stood beside it, and stretched upward on his hind legs, still watching and wagging. He followed something in the air to the highest corner of the ceiling, focusing on it. As his vision moved to the ceiling he paused momentarily, the wagging ceased and he turned to look at us.

I kept asking "What is it Trev? What do you see?" He just looked at us, then turned one last time and looked at the corner of the wall and ceiling. We did not see or hear anything. And then we got a chill.

Trevar had reacted the same way he always did whenever my mother came home. She was the only one he ever flattened his ears for. We were stunned as we realized the possibility of his vision.

As we questioned this sight openly, we could only come to one conclusion; Trevar welcomed Mom home just as he always had done—ears flat and tail wagging. We knew Mom had come home for one last time, and Trevar greeted her as always. He acknowledged her presence, and we are grateful to know she was with us.

Trevar gave us the gift of his vision that day, and a treasured sight for us to keep forever.

Dana Smith-Mansell

Wily

I think we are drawn to dogs because they are the uninhibited creatures we might be if we weren't certain we knew better.

George Bird Evans

When I was initially approached to write an article about a miniature schnauzer named Wily, one of the most singular personalities I have ever encountered, I was somewhat perplexed. Like many things one holds close to the chest, I rarely discuss him or his effect on me, and am generally uncomfortable doing so. How best to explain or account for the sixteen-plus years this unique character (and he was, truly, a character) graced the stage of my life?

I thought long and hard before agreeing to attempt what I'd often considered the impossible—describing the traits of a dog that, despite his diminutive stature, possessed a personality and zeal for life that rivaled that of the most animated and robust people I've encountered.

Wily was larger than life, a fifteen-pound tornado of black and salt-and-pepper fur, given to raising himself to challenges that seemed ridiculous, if not altogether outlandish, for him to take. Reflecting back on the life of this dear friend of mine, this trait often appears to me as the hallmark of his personality—despite his size and station in the world, he possessed no fear, and lived as if every day might be the last.

Oftentimes, his antics did raise some concern he was, in fact, in grave danger of not being long in the world. But whether by luck or the grace of God, he had a long life for a member of his breed, and I believe he enjoyed every day until the last. I admired and loved him dearly for his bravery and ability to squeeze every ounce of happiness out of the world he inhabited.

Wily came into my life, quite unexpectedly, as a birthday gift. I was turning ten, a rather austere age for those who, until then, have been nine. There is a weight to ten. There are two digits. One assumes a certain seriousness about his place in the world and future

92

prospects. At ten, we are no longer children. We are children who want desperately to be adults. Or at least, that was me, and my mother, recognizing this, presented me with two options for my birthday—a family vacation in Mexico, or a dog. Quite frankly, Mexico seemed more exciting.

But after careful consideration, I opted for the dog. I had recently become rather attached to Grizzly, a coal-black, champion-bred miniature schnauzer acquired some months prior by my eleven- and twelve-year-old first cousins. He was adorable, if a bit drowsy and cantankerous at times. He loved to play, for a few minutes at a time at least, and then would often assume the position of a large black doorstop for hours on end.

In essence, Grizzly was mostly calm and at times altogether unable to wake up, even as a puppy. Nonetheless, he and I had a fine relationship, and I eagerly anticipated a similar experience when my mom brought home a newly born half-brother of Grizzly's, all the way from a breeder in Delaware. Wily, however, would prove to be an altogether different personality type. I've heard it said schnauzers are more or less calm based on coloring, and I can't vouch for the veracity of this statement, but in the case of these two brothers, it was certainly the case.

Wily arrived on top of a deconstructed cardboard box in the back of my mother's yellow Subaru, looking plaintively up at me from that position as if to say, "Where am I and who the hell are you?" He was nervous, excitable, and excessively curious from Day One. It would be years and years before he could expend all of that nervous energy; and as far as the curiosity goes, that never left him.

On that first day, I held him, small as he was, securely in the palm of my ten-year-old hand, and he seemed simultaneously contented and indignant about this. He was clearly frightened to be away from the environment in which he was born, but at the same time, excited and eager to explore. Held aloft above the world on my hand, he looked searchingly around the house in which we stood, and gave me a look as if to say, "Very cute. Now put me down." I did, and he ran, exploring his new kingdom.

Those first six to twelve months, following that day, were a great deal of work for all of us, Wily included, in learning how to adjust to a newly configured family dynamic. He required, as all puppies do, copious amounts of attention in order to learn the basics. I hadn't figured on this. Our other dog, Pasha, was several years older than me, and Wily was the first dog I'd ever raised as a puppy.

Wily's training and upkeep was, by and large, my responsibility, and this changed my life significantly, giving me more of a taste for looking after the welfare of another creature than I had previously experienced. Puppies are a bit like babies, and I was just old enough, at the time Wily entered into my life, to be able to look after a baby with some degree of knowledge (and, admittedly, a good deal of help from my mother).

Wily was perpetually pushing the bounds of acceptable behavior. Looking after him required a great deal of patience, and gave me a lot of first-hand experience in learning to act as an advocate on behalf of another. I found myself in the dual role of disciplining and protecting him from the wrath of adults, as the case warranted. Conversations such as, "Mom, he didn't know those shoes were $200," or "I'm sorry Mrs. Burnett, he gets really excited about brightly colored flowers," became commonplace, as Wily, all ten or twelve pounds of him, increasingly became a jovial and mischievous personality who rarely went unnoticed. It was only a month or so into our time together that I decided on his name, having recognized these traits in him very early on.

Following those initial years of abject puppy-hood, Wily and I grew together in a similar fashion, bosom buddies in the first throes of adolescence and young adulthood. In addition to his curiosity and penchant for mischief-making, he developed a reputation as a fierce guardian around our neighborhood and among my friends. It became difficult for most people to get very close to me without him voicing some degree of displeasure, and not being very subtle about it either. His high-pitched barking and howling (he sounded very much like a small wolf at times) became a predictable indicator of someone being present at the door or in our front yard. If truly upset with someone,

Wily would adopt a low growl and scowling, slinking walk, as if to say, "I'm onto you, and don't try anything funny."

Over a period of years, I often found myself amazed at his ability to discern someone's character and act accordingly, usually before I was privy to it. I hesitate to anthropomorphosize animals in general, but this particular quality of his personality never ceased to amaze me. He was wise to something I still don't understand, even now. He could size people up based on the way they smelled, or so it seemed.

As I began to take an interest in girls in junior high and high school, Wily became increasingly skeptical of them, and let them know in no uncertain terms he was not interested in having them in my vicinity. He liked and sometimes didn't like my male friends, but as far as girls, he just didn't like them, period. He seemed to view them as a distraction from our playtime together, during which we would commonly spend hours on end, on long summer afternoons, running in the yard and woods, chasing squirrels, chipmunks, and tennis balls.

When I look back on my teenage years, I often view those times, and not the time made up of my boyhood love interests and other adolescent occupations, as among the finest of my life. If anything, I wish now I'd spent even more time running through the trees with him. He was quite fast for such a little dog. He loved to escape from the house at the slightest possible opportunity, wedging his way through a sliding glass door or half-cracked window. He seemed to enjoy it all the more when I would give chase behind him. On more than one occasion, he nearly outran me for several hundred yards or more. In short sprints, he was generally able to best me, much to my dismay. I made regional track finals several years in a row for longer races, and yet in a dead-on sprint, I was routinely ousted by a miniature schnauzer. He could run. His legs were small, but his determination and enthusiasm were huge.

With age and experience, Wily developed an increasing penchant for escaping from the house and exploring not only our immediate neighborhood, but also the several hundred acres of woods that made up a county park just a stone's throw from our front door. At times he would disappear for twenty-four hours or more, during which I would

95

worry to the point of sleeplessness, and which would inevitably end with his triumphant return, smelling of creek beds, damp leaves, and less mentionable things.

This was a schnauzer, mind you, not a Lab or a retriever. I felt he had no business spending nights in the wild, and yet he would do just that, and seemed to revel in it. I've heard schnauzers were bred by the Germans to hunt out rats and small pests from farms, and this instinct for pastoral recreation seemed strong in him. These proclivities, and his general fondness for new and pulse-quickening experiences, led him down some interesting paths during his adult years. Following are two such cases of Wily's intrepid adventures.

Upon my maternal grandmother's death in 1989, our house was flooded with family and food for a period of several days immediately following. As is generally the case, the occasion was filled with a heaviness and confusion among all parties involved. My mother's voluminous family came together in Northern Virginia, near our home, for the wake and funeral, and our house served as a sort of command-post central for the proceedings.

There was a great storm on the night of my grandmother's wake. The house and neighborhood were unusually dark, and no one seemed to think much about all of the food and drink that lay about the entire premises as we all traipsed out into a cold rain to attend this solemn event.

Wily, meanwhile, had been strategically testing his ability to move chairs and stools placed around the kitchen table. He'd been at this task for at least an hour before our departure, and I'd noticed him at it, but was ensconced in the same haze of emotion as the rest of my family, and his behavior hardly registered with me.

We returned home late that night to find a kitchen table emptied of the fresh-baked brownies that had occupied it earlier in the evening, and our beloved schnauzer in a state of frightening agitation and bewilderment. As many of us know, chocolate is in fact poisonous to dogs in even moderate amounts, depending on the size of the animal. Wily had consumed enough chocolate that night to sicken an adult human, let alone an animal of his size. There was no point in scolding him for it by the time we realized what had occurred. His punishment was already upon him.

Our primary concern was whether or not he would survive. I kept him close to me that night, and neither of us got much sleep. He was throwing up repeatedly, which we took as a good sign, while alternatingly bouncing off the walls (quite literally) and rolling on the floor. I held him close for a few moments at a time, before he could squirm out of my arms and continue his efforts at expelling all of that caffeinated delirium. I was alarmed to feel his heart racing against his chest.

He was sick for another few days thereafter, but managed to survive. We were always quite careful, thereafter, to keep all forms of chocolate completely out of his reach. Wily learned as an adult to open doors and move light pieces of furniture, so there always was a bit of an ongoing vigilance required to ensure he not be able to reach food he shouldn't eat. As was often the case with Wily's antics, the incident left me feeling simultaneously impressed by his prowess and determination, and exasperated by his disregard for the limits of physics and biology. But, so it always went with him. I've heard from others dogs will often eat to the point of bursting and beyond, for reasons we humans can't quite fathom.

Several years thereafter, on a bright spring evening in my junior year of high school, Wily and I were out taking a routine walk in the neighborhood, with him on a leash and, in typical fashion, trying his best to out-power and out-distance this leash. He was always eager to run two steps beyond any sort of confine you might place upon him, and walking on a leash was no exception. Not until I was grown, more or less, into the body I would inhabit as an adult, was I strong and agile enough to ensure he would not somehow manage to break away from me during our walks, leash or no leash.

On this particular evening, towards the top of a long incline of tree-lined asphalt toward the top of our neighborhood, we came across an unleashed Alaskan husky, a neighbor's dog of great stature and calm demeanor I'd frequently seen and interacted with previously, largely without event or incident. He was a good-natured, gentle giant with ice-blue eyes and a friendly swagger to his step.

Upon encountering Wily, he nonchalantly approached and attempted to initiate the typical greeting ritual among dogs, marked by sniffing and circling of both anterior and posterior.

Wily, for whatever reason, was in no mood for such formalities on this particular evening, and immediately began growling and positioned himself to pounce. In retrospect, I realized he was probably intimidated by this much larger animal, and felt the need to protect and defend. The husky was slow to react, not quite even recognizing the situation initially. But after thirty or forty-five seconds of this, during which I and the husky's owner both felt reasonably assured we were in control of the situation and this would subside once the two dogs adjusted to each other's presence, the husky became visibly upset and began growling as well.

Now, as a caveat in explaining this story, I should mention Wily was raised around, and spent most of his life with, two dogs much larger than him—our older dog Pasha, a mixed-breed mutt about twice Wily's size, and our next-door-neighbor's golden retriever, Maddie, who was at least four times the size of Wily. Wily was no stranger to larger dogs, and ultimately understood his place in the pecking order. As such, I figured he would calm down after a few moments in the husky's presence. I'd also witnessed the little-dog-versus-big-dog phenomenon enough over time to recognize in general, while larger dogs are generally slower to react and grow agitated, once they do, a smaller dog that was initially aggressive may well come to his senses and run for cover.

As the husky grew upset, Wily took the opposite approach. While moments before I'd felt sure the situation would blow over, within seconds of the husky's growling, Wily lunged, schnauzer jaws wide open for the kill, and planted himself firmly upon the husky's mane, just below the neck. From that precarious post, Wily hung on for dear life as the husky shook to free himself of this pint-size attacker and both his owner and I stood looking on in total disbelief.

No one knew quite what to do, including the dogs. Wily hung from this animal's shoulder, in a tenacious vice-grip, or as much of a tenacious vice-grip as a miniature schnauzer can muster. The husky's owner and I stood looking on, horrified and in disbelief. The husky himself was completely shocked. He just stood there, as if trying to comprehend the ridiculousness of the situation. He didn't appear to be in any pain. His previous agitation had morphed into complete confusion. He looked up at me with an expression of dismay, as if to say, "What the hell kind of schnauzer is this?"

Realizing the husky was now thoroughly confused and not reacting violently, I gingerly approached, and began to disentangle Wily from the upper body of this creature who could easily have had him for lunch. After some prodding and pressure, during which the husky thankfully stood still and remained calm, I was able to remove Wily.

Ultimately, there was no harm done. The husky seemed fine. Wily had proven his point, but hadn't managed to even draw blood. We all left the scene, slightly embarrassed and uncertain as to what had just occurred. Wily, throughout his life, was often brave to the point of stupidity. He was tough, tenacious, and not to be belittled, despite his size. On this particular occasion, he was damn lucky he hadn't encountered a large dog with a less forgiving attitude.

There were many more eventful days and nights in our time together, too many to recount here. Time passed, as it does. I grew up and left for school, and Wily became a part of home, a familiar old friend whom I'd see every few months. I noticed certain tell-tale signs of his aging, but eventually grew less concerned, and frankly, less aware, of these. I recall distinctly, when Wily turned twelve (at which point I was twenty-two), feeling a genuine angst and fear of his impending departure from the world. This passed, and with each subsequent year I was lulled into a false sense of his permanence that I suspect proves common among pet owners.

In the fall of 2001, Wily grew increasingly slow and calm. I was back from college, working in the Washington, D.C. area and living at home again, and so was witness to this change I might otherwise not have noticed as fully. He would sometimes sleep for seven or eight hours at a stretch. It was an unseasonably warm autumn, and I would often find him splayed out in a sunbeam, snoring contentedly, his scarred nose (from an altercation with a neighbor's cat, some ten years prior) as cold and wet as ever. He seemed healthy and simply mellowing with age. At times during that fall, he would sleep by my side throughout the night. But not in the old way to which I'd grown accustomed as a teenager, whereby we would repeatedly jostle throughout the night, with him wanting to plant his torso firmly on top of my head, subsequently preventing me from breathing. In those days of 2001, he would instead sleep nestled up against my side, the length of his body still beneath the covers, burrowed into me.

Several days before Christmas of that year, my father and I left to visit family in upstate New York for the holidays. On a cold, crisp morning we went out to take Wily for a walk, in the pre-dawn hours, before catching a cab to the airport. He was unusually chipper and alert that morning, and seemed particularly excited, which surprised me, given his usual reaction to my leaving was one of sulking and reserve. He'd seen the suitcases for several days prior, and so I expected he would react as he always had. But he didn't. Instead he was happy and energetic, bounding down the steps and out the door into the cold in a manner reminiscent of his younger days.

We walked under a clear winter sky, filled with stars that were quite bright, watching our breath fill the chasm of December air at 3 a.m. We took him back indoors and headed off on our trip. I never saw him again.

Several days later, on Christmas morning, my mother informed me of his passing. She didn't want to tell me, it was Christmas morning after all, but I knew something had happened, and so she acquiesced and informed me.

It all happened suddenly, it seems. His hind legs gave out, and it was the end. There was no indication of this in the weeks prior, or perhaps I just didn't notice. He really was happy and energetic until the end. This seems common with dogs. I'm grateful he didn't suffer any protracted sickness.

And I've often thought to myself, "What good would it have done to have known that was it?" He lived a good long life, and I felt perhaps he was happy to know we were headed off somewhere on that morning because, knowing Wily, he would have never wanted to leave us behind.

John Cali III

In Loving Memory of Tote

The love of a dog is unconditional, unwavering, and helps us remember who we really are, and to know we are loved. No greater gift has ever been given.

Unknown

Tote was a tiny three-month-old pup when we first saw him in Pine Ridge, South Dakota. Half coyote mixed with husky and shepherd, Tote was a striking mutt. He resembled a black hairless piglet; yet, it was love at first sight. He had beautiful blue eyes, hence, the name "Tote" which means "blue" in Lakota. Tote was one of two puppies of Katherine Red Feather, whose eyes were also blue when she was a child. After completing Katherine's home[8], she gave us Tote as a gift.

Before leaving the open grassland of Pine Ridge, Tote caught a big fat toad, which he ate contentedly as he likely did on many a day on the reservation. But after arriving in urbanite Bellevue, Washington, he was fed the finest dog food money could buy, Costco-size. We even moved to a rental house so Tote would have a yard. Well, actually, we were told to vacate our studio apartment just a month after Tote's arrival when he was heard howling like a coyote on our deck.

Tote then attended a prestigious doggy academy and underwent intense training on how to sit, heel, lie down, and not jump on people—all of which he forgot how to do within three months. But that wasn't all he could *not* do. Upon training Tote to catch a Frisbee® or ball, he was fantastic at following the object with his eyes but then would allow the object to hit him square on his forehead. "Good dog!" we encouraged.

---

[8] The author, Robert Young, is the founder and executive director of Red Feather Development Group which builds homes for American Indians in Washington, Montana, and South Dakota.

When our daughter Skylar arrived, she turned our world upside down. Tote especially felt the shift: no more daily walks, no more play. All Tote heard was, "Coo-chi, coo-chi, coo!" As Skylar grew and started walking, Tote began to receive attention again, but now it was from small hands pulling on his fur, placing pebbles on his head, poking his eyes, or being pulled on a leash and walked around and around and around and around. Sweet patient Tote! He would look at us pleadingly, as if he were saying, "Could you get this little person away from me?"

Tote will be missed dearly, but his spirit will forever be in our hearts. Rest in peace, sweet Tote. We love you.

Tote Young, born June 1995, deceased October 2006. He was born on the Pine Ridge Reservation in South Dakota. Survivors are Robert, Anita, and Skylar Young. Interests were sleeping, going to the Red Feather office, guarding the office hallway, begging for doggy treats from office neighbors, and sleeping.

Robert O. Young

Through the Eyes of Love

An animal's eyes have the power to speak a great language.
Martin Buber

Last Saturday, after a meeting with two of my friends, we had an experience that transcends words. It still lingers in my heart, with great gratitude for having had it at all. To tell the story does not seem out of the ordinary, except it was extraordinary—as love always is.

After our meeting, we went to a restaurant, and as we got out of the car, a woman on a bike rode by. She asked if we had any change. I only had a $20 bill, which was for dinner, so I said "No."

She rode off, and one of my friends commented on her cute dog, in her bike carrier. I called out to the bicyclist, she stopped, and we went to see the dog. We noticed immediately there was a depth of quality in the woman's presence. She was like a friend, someone we had known for a long time.

She shared that her dog was fifteen years old, and had cancer. She told us the dog had been stolen twice, and she prayed so hard for its return. God answered her prayers.

She talked about being homeless, but did not seem unhappy about it. I think she said she lived in her car. I looked into the dog's eyes and, truly, they became the eyes of Christ.

Really they did. They were large and full of light. I stared into them and said, in my heart, "Oh my God—you are so beautiful!"

Before the thought was finished, the dog leaped from the basket, right into my arms, and licked my face.

After a few minutes, the dog began to shake a little. So the woman got off her bike, opened up a bag, and pulled out pajamas for the dog. She took him, sat on the ground, and lovingly put on his pajamas.

The love between her and the dog was heart-warming. She gently put him back into the basket, and we continued to talk.

We could have stayed forever in that moment, as time stopped, and we were just in the deliciousness of it all. It felt like a holy encounter for all of us.

I searched my purse again, found $5, and handed it to our mystery lady. My friend also found $5 she did not realize she had.

As the woman rode away, she turned to me and said "Happy Birthday. You will live to be very old." None of us had told her it was any of our birthdays. We stood there stunned!

My friends and I all felt this woman was very special, and we were blessed by her presence. I have never before in my life felt face-to-face with God, in the eyes of a dog. I truly was overwhelmed by the beauty in this dog's eyes.

And it was my 70th birthday!

The encounter was a special gift, as I love animals!

Marie Rhodes

Who Is John Cali?

John Cali has loved dogs almost all his life. For many years, he's had a parade of canine characters frolicking through his life.

A freelance writer since 1986, John has written for magazines, newspapers, newsletters, and other publications. He has published ten books and several newsletters on various topics, including business and spirituality. In addition to his writing, John also does spiritual counseling.

John, originally from western New York State, now lives in a remote area of northwestern Wyoming, just outside Yellowstone National Park, amidst assorted critters, domestic and wild.

Contact John at:

P.O. Box 442
Cody, WY 82414
USA
Email: john@greatwesternpublishing.org
Web site: http://www.greatwesternpublishing.org

Contributors

Judith Anderson is a photographer and writer specializing in archaeological and sacred sites, mostly in Central and South America. She is also currently owned by two dogs, Tsunami and Amaru, and two cats, Raphael and Miranda, all of whom have stories of their own.

Betti Bernardi is a freelance writer with a background in behavioral science. Her articles, poetry, and short stories are published in a variety of publications. She recently completed a book of poetry.

Robert Paul Blumenstein lives in Richmond, Virginia with his wife and miniature schnauzer, Fitzgerald. He earned an MFA from Virginia Commonwealth University in play writing. Many of his short stories have been published in national publications, and recently his story, "The Spanish Piano," appeared in the international journal, *The Taj Mahal Review*. Also, he has published a novel, *Flirtin' with Jesus*, a quirky thriller. His second novel, *Snapping the String*, was published October 1, 2007.

Noreen Braman, author of *I'm 50—Now What?* is a writer from Jamesburg, New Jersey who has published poetry, fiction, humor, non-fiction, and horror in large and small presses. She was the editor of *Images of America: Milltown*, a historical photo book published by Arcadia Press. She has won numerous writing awards and is the single mother of three adult children who think she is the funniest mother they know. Her website is *http://www.lulu.com/noreenbraman*.

Renie Burghardt is a freelance writer who was born in Hungary. Her work has appeared in many anthologies, including *Chicken Soup for the Soul* books, *Cup of Comfort*, *GuidepostsBooks*, *Rocking Chair Reader*, *Chocolate for Women*, and many others. She lives in the country and loves nature, animals, hiking in the woods, spending time on the river, and enjoying the company of her family and friends. Get in touch with her at: *renie_burghardt@yahoo.com*.

John Cali III is a native of the Washington, D.C. area, and completed his undergraduate degree at New York University before working for several years as a consultant and engineer in the information technology and financial services sectors. He served with his wife as a Peace Corps Volunteer in Zambia, and is currently a graduate student in business at The University of North Carolina at Chapel Hill. He rarely writes anything lengthier than an email.

Cathy Clamp is a freelance writer and author from the Texas hill country. She has published more than twenty outdoor (hunting/fishing) feature articles for national magazines, several articles for legal trade journals, short stories, newspaper articles, plus six co-authored paranormal romance novels with Tor Books. Cathy is now an award-winning USA Today best-selling author.

Susan Dennis lives on the Gold Coast in Queensland, Australia on an acreage property with her English setters and horses. She has always had a great love for, and deep spiritual connection with animals and nature since childhood, maybe since she was born. Susan's Web site is *http://www.findingbeau.com* and her email address is *susan@findingbeau.com*.

Susanne Fogle has written a weekly newspaper column about animals and environmental issues for nine years. She has recently completed her first book, *Animal Tails: A Guide to Loving, Respecting and Coping with the Animals in Our Lives*. She is also a contributor to the *Chicken Soup for the Soul* books. You can contact her agent, Dr. Uwe Stender, at *uwe@triadaus.com* or email her at *Susannefogle@AOL.com*.

Kate Fratti, 48, is a national award-winning columnist for the daily Bucks County Courier Times in Pennsylvania. Married twenty-six years, she's the mother of two grown kids, a daughter now living in Rome, and a son who is a U.S. Marine stationed at Camp LeJeune. That leaves her doting on a pit bull.

Wolf Halton is a writer and educator, living in the Atlanta, Georgia area. He worked in the pet-care industry for fifteen years and currently runs a company that assists the owners of start-ups to succeed so they don't end up in the doghouse or the poorhouse. Wolf Halton, *saphil@yahoo.com.*

Nancy Ilk lives in Oak Creek, Wisconsin with her husband, Jim, and their yellow Lab, Gracie. When not writing, Nancy enjoys long walks through the woods with Gracie. When she's not walking or writing, she's reading, reading, reading. Her stories and essays have appeared in *Happy Woman Magazine, Healing Woman, Pet Stories* (Shirley MacLaine Web site), and other online publications. Her essay, "Beyond the Madness," appears in Yitta Hammerstam's recently published anthology, *Changing Course.*

Dana Smith-Mansell is the author of the children's book *Stop Bullying Bobby*, writer and illustrator of *Visions of Existence* (poetry & art), *Sacred Intentions* (poetry), and one of six co-authors of the inspirational title, *Pink Jasper: Gems from the Journey.* Her work has appeared in various print, Web, and greeting card publications. Dana has a bachelor's degree in special education, a master's degree in behavior disorders, and resides at the base of a mountain in Pennsylvania, amid nature, with her four terriers, cat, and husband.

Walter McElligott is a freelance writer living in south suburban Chicago, a ghostwriter for a Chicago lawyer, an author of Chicagoland history and travel articles for local newspapers, and an e-zine story on his wife Joan's healing from breast cancer. Walter's story, "Memories in the Making," was published in the anthology, *Cup of Comfort for Weddings* at Christmas 2006. He also has an e-book, *A Blessed Bethlehem Birth*, published by Guardian Angel Publishing (*http://www.guardianangelpublishing.com)* at Christmas 2007. Walter is also editor of the Chicago Writers' Association's *Clarion Newsletter.*

Marie Rhodes has an AA degree in child development. She has been a Head Start teacher, and started the first center in California for chronically and terminally ill children. At present, her life's purpose is serving people who are awakening spiritually. Marie teaches *A Course in Miracles*, and is a devotee of the spiritual master, Meher Baba. She considers prayer and extending love to her fellow humans her greatest work, a work she practices daily.

EDITOR'S NOTE: *We wish to thank Mary Ellen of Angel Scribe®, at http://www.angelscribe.com, for bringing Marie's story to our attention.*

The River & Plains Society is a nonprofit group dedicated to preserving and providing education about the history of Chouteau County, Montana and the surrounding areas. It also operates the Museum of the Northern Great Plains, the Museum of the Upper Missouri, and the Old Fort Benton. Contact them at P.O. Box 262, Fort Benton, MT 59442-0262 USA, or at their Fort Benton Web site, *http://www.fortbenton.com/museums/index.htm*. The article "Forever Faithful: Shep's Story" on page 46 is partially based on the booklet, *Forever Faithful: The Story of Shep*. Copies of the booklet are available from the River and Plains Society.

Gayle Trent is a full-time freelance writer, author, editor, publisher, chief cook and bottle washer, wife and last, but certainly not least, mom. Her most recent novel *When Good Bras Go Bad* is now available from Grace Abraham Publishing. Learn more about Gayle at *http://gayle24202.tripod.com*.

Anne C. Watkins is the author of *The Conure Handbook* and is a contributing editor to *Pet Age Magazine*. Her animal stories have appeared in books such as *Chicken Soup for the Dog Lover's Soul* and in eight volumes of the *GuidepostsBooks* series, *Listening to the Animals*. She and her husband Allen live in rural Alabama amidst a myriad of animals and birds.

Elaine Whitesides is a confirmed dachshund owner living between Michigan and Indiana. She appreciates the beauty, charm, and grace of the dachshund, as well as the individual personalities and quirky behaviors she doesn't always understand. Dachshunds Eric, Kelly, Cleo, and Sarah were Simon's predecessors. Each was unique, but none prepared her for life with nervous-bellied, deaf, fourteen-year-old Simon. With a strong stomach and poor sleeping patterns, she meets all the requirements for the job of caretaker to Simon. Despite his idiosyncrasies, Elaine and Simon are traveling companions who frequently traverse roads through the prairies of the Midwest. She writes and he gives her material. It is a good match for both of them.

Robert O. Young is the founder and executive director of Red Feather Development Group in Bozeman, Montana. Seven years ago, Robert, then a clothing manufacturer, read a newspaper article about elderly American Indians freezing in their own homes. That led to Robert's dream of building homes for them. The dream started with building one home, for Katherine Red Feather, and grew into an organization named in her honor. Today, Red Feather builds homes on reservations across Washington, Montana, and South Dakota. You can contact Red Feather Development Group at P.O. Box 907, Bozeman, MT 59771-0907 USA or at their Web site, *http://www.redfeather.org*.

Copyright Permissions

Resources

Join us in supporting these worthy organizations that do so much for the well-being of dogs and all animals

Pets for Life program of the Humane Society of the United States (HSUS): http://www.PetsForLife.org and http://www.hsus.org. The goal of the Pets for Life program is to curtail the numbers of animals relinquished to shelters—or otherwise given up on—because of breaks in the human-animal bond.

Therapy Dogs International, Inc.: http://www.tdi-dog.org. Therapy Dogs International, Inc. (TDI) is a volunteer organization dedicated to the regulating, testing, and registration of therapy dogs and their volunteer handlers for the purpose of visiting nursing homes, hospitals, other institutions, and wherever else therapy dogs are needed.

Petfinder: http://www.petfinder.com. This is the temporary home of 256,054 adoptable pets from 10,835 adoption groups.

Pets911.com is another organization that searches for homeless pets and makes them available for adoption. http://www.1888pets911.org.

American Kennel Club Breed Rescue Groups is a clearinghouse for homeless pets available for adoption. The listings are by breed so potential adopters can narrow their possible selections to the breed they want. Web site: http://www.akc.org/breeds/rescue.cfm.

Greenpeople.org is an alphabetical listing of humane societies, animal shelters, and pet adoption organizations by US state and city, Canadian province, and other countries. Their Web site is here: http://www.greenpeople.org/humanesociety.htm.

Additional Resources

One of the saddest things about having a dog in your life is the near-certainty he or she will die before you.

I've dealt with the deaths of my beloved dogs over many years now. When Blackie, my first dog, died just two days before Christmas, there was nearly no understanding or compassion from my family for the deep sadness I felt. In fact, one family member, on Christmas Day, criticized my feelings with the comment, "He was just a dog."

Today, fortunately, there are more resources available for grieving pet owners than there were back then. Here are a few I recommend.

The Rainbow Bridge: http://www.rainbowbridge.org. This is a beautifully compassionate Web site where, for no charge, you can post a memorial for your beloved pet.

The American Veterinary Medical Association (AVMA): http://www.avma.org. AVMA has some great resources for grieving pet owners. Simply go to their site, and insert the phrase "when your animal dies" into their search engine.

Pet Loss Grief Support Web site: http://www.petloss.com. Petloss.com has a wealth of resources for grieving pet owners, including personal support, thoughtful advice, The Monday Pet Loss Candle Ceremony, tribute pages, healing poetry, and more.

Chance's Spot: http://www.chancesspot.org. Chance's Spot is a 501(c)(3) nonprofit organization dedicated to supporting individuals who have suffered the loss of a dearly loved pet.

There are many more caring, compassionate organizations like these. To find them, go to http://www.google.com and do a search on the phrase "grieving for a pet." (Omit the period at the end.) You'll find thousands of references.

Finally, here are some books for anyone, young or old, grieving the death of a pet:

Animals and the Afterlife: True Stories of Our Best Friends' Journey Beyond Death and *Animals and the Afterlife, Book 2: The Journey Continues*, both by Kim Sheridan.

Pet Loss: A Thoughtful Guide for Adults and Children by Herbert A. Nieburg.

When Your Pet Dies: How to Cope with Your Feelings by Jamie Quackenbush and Denise Graveline.

Coping with Sorrow on the Loss of Your Pet by Moira K. Anderson.

The Loss of a Pet by Wallace Sife.

Coping with the Loss of a Pet by Christina M. Lemieux and Denis G. Lemay.

These books are especially for children coping with a pet's loss:

Charlotte's Web by E. B. White and Garth Williams.

The Tenth Good Thing About Barney by Judith Viorst and Erik Blegvad.

Oh, Where Has My Pet Gone?: A Pet Loss Memory Book, Ages 3-103 by Sally Sibbitt.

EDITOR'S NOTE: All the above books were available at *http://www.amazon.com* when we last checked. Amazon also has many other books on the same subjects.

A Final Story

On a final note, I recently heard a deeply touching little story, source unknown, about a six-year old boy whose elderly dog had to be put down. He and his parents watched as their veterinarian helped the dog slip peacefully and quietly away.

When it was done, the adults sat around talking for a few minutes about the shortness of animals' lives. They were surprised at how calm the boy was.

Noticing their inquiring glances, the boy said he knew why animals lived such short lives. He said humans lived long lives because they needed to learn how to be good and loving. Dogs already know that, he said. So they don't need to live as long.

John Cali

How to Order More Copies of This Book

If you wish to order more copies of this book, either as an e-book or as a printed copy, you can get them online at BookLocker.com or you can order printed copies through your favorite online or brick and mortar bookstore.